PHILOSOPHY OF PHENOMENA

BY

GEORGE M. RAMSEY, M. D.

AUTHOR OF "COSMOLOGY"

IN TWO PARTS

I. METAPHYSICAL PHENOMENA

II. PHYSICAL PHENOMENA

Error always promotes evil, Truth always promotes good; therefore, try all things, and cast away everything that fails to prove true.

BOSTON
BANNER OF LIGHT PUBLISHING CO.
1897

Copyright, 1896,
By GEORGE M. RAMSEY.

S. J. PARKHILL & CO., PRINTERS, BOSTON, MASS.

To my

BROTHER WILLIAM,

TWELVE YEARS FROM FLESH DEPARTED,

𝔗𝔥𝔦𝔰 𝔙𝔬𝔩𝔲𝔪𝔢

IS AFFECTIONATELY DEDICATED.

June 30, 1892.

PREFACE.

In introducing this book, the author perceives difficulty in writing an appropriate preface, free from arrogance, sycophantia and egoism. Herein all phenomena are classified as physical and metaphysical (matter phenomena and life phenomena). The cosmic forces of gravity, heat and life are recognized as chief factors of all phenomena.

The author deeply regrets that new departures of thought arouse bitter animosity. Intolerance of new ideas, leading to higher culture, has made the past lurid with flame and crimsoned with blood. Honest belief, however, is no evidence of truth; but honest research will eventually lead to its discovery. Ignorance is the mother of cruelty, in all forms. Knowledge alone works goodness.

The age of reason tarries. The *ipse dixit* of the dark ages governs, bearing the fruits of indiscriminate pillage and massacre, as of yore. Alas! every Christian nation on earth, instigated by avarice, is, under some moral or gospel pretext, engaged in pillage and murder of weaker and less fortunate nations.

The cowardice of men, arising from fear of an imaginary superior, begets cruelty; while the evolution of civilization, dimly recognized, has demonstrated that honesty, industry and kindness fulfil all there is, or ever was, of law and gospel, and are amply sufficient to make everybody good and happy evermore.

Lest the reader's feelings be offended at tautological blurs herein, the author begs to say that innovations always beget antagonism. Therefore it becomes imperative to embrace every opportunity offered to explain the new, from every point of view. Hence the repetitions, with regrets. Further is not insisted by the AUTHOR.

CONTENTS.

PART I.—METAPHYSICAL PHENOMENA.

CHAPTER		PAGE
I.	Philosophy of Phenomena,	9
II.	Metaphysical Philosophy,	14
III.	Heat,	18
IV.	Functional Phenomena,	25
V.	Man,	34
VI.	Objective and Subjective Phenomena,	41
VII.	"Who by Searching Can Find God?"	45
VIII.	Hyperbole Metaphysical,	47
IX.	"To the Unknown God, whom ye Ignorantly Worship,"	51
X.	"The Father is Greater than I,"	53
XI.	True and Spurious Gods,	55
XII.	"I am the Resurrection and the Life,"	58
XIII.	An Imaginary God and Some of his Exploits,	61
XIV.	"He is Free, whom the Truth hath Made Free,"	68
XV.	All Animates Originate from Eggs,	70
XVI.	Trance Phenomenon,	71
XVII.	Philosophy of Healing,	75
XVIII.	Worship of Deity,	79
XIX.	Sense and Nonsense Intermixed,	80
XX.	Plurality and Tri-Unity of God,	83

CHAPTER		PAGE
XXI.	Vagaries,	88
XXII.	Misapprehension,	89
XXIII.	What is Sin?	93
XXIV.	Suns, Planets and Satellites of the Universe,	99
XXV.	Beginning without Ending,	104
XXVI.	Design or Accident, Which?	106
XXVII.	Chance versus Law,	111
XXVIII.	Summary,	118

PART II.—PHYSICAL PHENOMENA.

XXIX.	Nebulæ,	120
XXX.	Air Pressure, and Air Motion, as a Motor,	132
XXXI.	Air, and Orbital Motions,	134
XXXII.	Water Made to Run up Hill,	162
XXXIII.	Philosophy of Canons: When and How Formed,	165
XXXIV.	Glacial Phenomena,	172
XXXV.	Moons and Their Motions,	182
XXXVI.	Ethnological Phenomena,	186
XXXVII.	The Colored Man,	195

APPENDIX.

Problems,	199
Physical and Metaphysical Phenomena, ad infinitum,	205

PHILOSOPHY OF PHENOMENA.

PART I.

METAPHYSICAL PHENOMENA.

CHAPTER I.

PHILOSOPHY OF PHENOMENA.

PHENOMENA include every manifestation of nature.

Hitherto nature has been divided into three general divisions: the mineral, the vegetable and the animal.

The subject has further been divided into the physical and the metaphysical phenomena.

Between these latter two classes there is an intermediate class that may be called either semi-physical or semi-metaphysical.

Again, all phenomena may for convenience be designated as life phenomena and matter phenomena, wherein life is not manifested, as contradistinguished from phenomena wherein life is manifested.

All phenomena are included within these latter two classes.

In the first three general divisions we find the mineral blend with the vegetable and the vegetable blend with the animal, so as to render the exact line that marks the divisions difficult of perception.

Physical phenomena result only from the reciprocal and antagonistic reaction of physical elements and forces inherent in matter.

Metaphysical phenomena result from the combined action of life and mind upon matter.

Semi-physical phenomena result from the union of life and matter as manifested in vegetable.

All phenomena are natural.

No unnatural phenomena.

No supernatural phenomena.

Nature is a full store of all phenomena that ever did or ever can occur.

Outside of nature, nothing.

Or, in other words, nature has no outside; neither centre nor circumference.

Phenomena are facts.

Philosophy not founded on fact is fallacious.

In surveying this vast field, we find phenomena that give no clue to origin.

However, if such phenomena be carefully scrutinized, a philosophy may be elaborated therefrom, that leads to conclusions relative thereto, that are almost as reliable as demonstrative evidence; for example, —

Life and matter are phenomena, are facts.

All scientific experiments, all logical deductions therefrom show that life and matter are indestructible; consequently are self-existent, from all eternity to all eternity. Hence all forces inherent in matter and all attributes inherent in life are self-existent.

Thence it follows, that these premises are not assumptions, but are logical deductions from a scientific basis.

The self-existence of life and matter, including all their attributes, is no more marvellous than their non-existence would be.

To be is not more strange than not to be.

Life and matter are the *first two* phenomena, are the sole factors of all phenomena, are the two factors from which all subsequent phenomena become possible.

Therefore, our first inquiries are: What is life? What is matter?

Their nature, their possibilities preclude a definite answer; but may be proximately defined by ascertaining their many attributes, all of which are known by manifestations.

In elaborating a philosophy of any phenomenon, perplexities inevitably arise.

Many of which are due to illogical deductions, and an inordinate desire to embrace more than logical deductions warrant.

If authors could be contented with knowledge that is demonstrable or logically deductive, avoiding the transcendental, the absurd and ridiculous, nine-tenths of all perplexities that arise would never appear or would quickly vanish.

When any phenomenon under consideration is not demonstrable, the mode of investigation should be so conducted that conclusions arrived at should be logically in harmony with conclusions made from similar phenomena that are demonstrable.

Thence we must give such a definition of life and matter that each may be relegated to its own proper plane and value, in order that each may become an exponent of other phenomena that otherwise would be wholly inexplicable.

Our first remark is that life manifests only in three forms, namely, germination, animation and mind.

From these arise an infinite variety of phenomena.

Now, as something can never come from nothing, it follows that though life in the abstract is a unit, yet it is a component of infinite attributes, each and all of which can only manifest through matter.

Thence the answer comes, that *life* is that which *manifests life phenomena* through matter; whilst matter is that by and through which life phenomena and physical phenomena are manifested.

Strictly speaking, matter is never germinated or animated; it is only used by life for manifestations.

The whole domain of phenomena is embraced within these premises.

Without matter, we could have no knowledge of life.

Without life, we could have no knowledge of matter.

Although the universe be filled therewith, all would be as naught.

Again, without either life or matter, knowledge would not have existed, could not have originated.

Knowledge is evolved from life, consequent upon the union of life with matter in organic form.

Matter alone never evolves intelligence.

Matter implies and includes all the constituent elements, and all the inherent forces by which it is actuated, apart from life.

All physical phenomena are produced by these inherent forces, unaided by life.

Life implies and includes mind. Mind is one of life's attributes.

Mind includes all intellectual and all sensational phenomena.

The organic union of life with matter is a prerequisite of all life phenomena.

Life is the originating impulse to all life phenomena.

Matter is constituted of subtle elements easily acted upon by the more subtle forces inherent therein; consequently, is constantly undergoing a change in its elementary relations.

Life in the abstract is unchangeable.

But, in its relations to matter it is ever evolving new phenomena, consequent upon the ceaseless changing of matter in its atomic relations.

Life through matter develops an infinite variety of attributes in kind and degree.

Every attribute manifested, results from environment; environment is the result of inherent forces of life and matter, and must of necessity harmonize with these forces.

A silly idea, borrowed from the fakirs of India, has taken possession of a few shallow thinkers, namely, that matter has no real existence. A brief analysis of this fad shows its idiocy.

If it is an axiom, that something never comes from nothing, it follows, that if matter had no existence, mind could not beget or entertain a thought of its existence or non-existence.

'Tis the fact of its existence that begets the thought of it.

Mind being a latent attribute of life — both requiring matter for expression ere the existence of either becomes known — how ludicrous it is to deny the existence of that by which alone we gain a knowledge of existence.

The fakirs are an abnormal people.

A long and persistent effort to subdue the flesh has succeeded to a degree that renders them abnormal whether in or out of the flesh.

Hence their distorted views of matter.

CHAPTER II.

METAPHYSICAL PHILOSOPHY.

METAPHYSICAL philosophy is the special delight and perplexity of many thinkers.

As we proceed in the investigation of the philosophy of phenomena, a clear apprehension of this so-called science becomes desirable, especially when considering the relation of mind to matter, together with the relation of the visible to the invisible realities.

This philosophy at the present day comprises three schools: realism, idealism and scepticism.

At the outset we submit, that, if life and matter are self-existent, co-eternal, ubiquitous throughout unlimited space, something could not exist outside of space, or disconnected from life and matter; that, if we comprehend the whole by the term nature, in its fullest and broadest sense, we thus learn that outside of and disconnected from nature there is nothing.

Thence, if we apply the old familiar theorem, that something can never come from nothing, and add that other truism that nothing has no existence, we inevitably arrive at the conclusion that all that is, is real; that all idealism is possible realism, has realism for its basis; that fiction *per se* has no existence; that a lie is only the exaggeration of truth; that thought is as real and as natural as life and matter, although it can neither be seen, heard, weighed nor measured; that all vagaries of the mind, all myths, all folk lore arise from imperceptible and imperfect mental impressions, all of which had their origin from and were suggested by nature.

Kith or kin, friends and foes, ofttimes give us mental impressions unperceived by us.

Intoxicants and narcotics are agents that produce favorable conditions for mental impresses of thought, resulting in the wildest extravaganza — as spooks, fairies, Tam O'Shanters, and and one woman sitting on seven hills, etc.

Scepticism arises from ignorance, from not knowing a sufficient number of facts relative to the matter under consideration, together with the lack of ability to logically connect facts whereby logical deductions lead to reliable conclusions.

This is all there is of scepticism, therefore requires no further consideration.

Every phenomenon of nature becomes possible of demonstration, inasmuch as the agencies by which all are produced exist in nature and will ever remain a full store of all.

It is the grasping after the supernatural that has so long clogged the progress of knowledge; and so long as man persists in mystifying nature by ignoring phenomena as natural, by imputing such to supernatural causes, so long will he fail to realize knowledge founded on facts, and so long will be unable to deduce a philosophy founded on facts.

The terms supernatural and supermundane are misleading.

We have seen that everything exists within, instead of outside of, nature; thence the term supernatural is wholly inadmissible; in point of fact there is no supernatural in the universe.

Words, in all languages, have no meaning except only that which is delegated to them by those who use them.

Now, inasmuch as many words have arisen from an exaggeration, from an inaccurate comprehension of things, it follows that when the false conceptions have been eradicated the terms formerly applied thereto become misnomers; therefore the term supermundane is wholly inapplicable when used to designate phenomena that occur within the earth's sphere (including her atmosphere), that the term can only be applied to phenomena that occur on celestial bodies exterior to and distant from the earth and her atmosphere.

When the earth's mass is weighed as against other planets,

her atmosphere is always included; hence, strictly speaking, in the definite language of science, we can have no supermundane phenomena of life on earth, relative either to the past, present or future.

In a limited sense we have two mundane spheres: the visible and invisible spheres, the spheres of earth and air.

We should ever avoid the indefinite and mystic realm suggested by the term spirit world. Spirit is wholly void of matter.

It requires matter to constitute a world.

Spirit world to many means a supernatural world. Surely there is no supernatural world.

And yet we find a learned ignoramus, who has exhausted the alphabet to designate his many high-sounding titles, devoting a large volume in explanation of *natural laws* operating in a *supernatural world*.

How nonsensical!

Again, spirit and soul are terms that are much abused. To many they are synonymous, whilst to others they are different.

Neither should ever be used to designate anything palpable. Spirit body is a misnomer, spirit is imponderable, incorporeal, is immaterial, is void of body.

Spirit is impalpable and its only logical meaning is life, and when thus used never becomes misleading.

Not being a philologist, we may not venture to coin a new word for spirit, but we are privileged to restrict its sense to a definite meaning.

Spirit is life, and life is natural — ever was, and ever will be.

Life, apart from matter, is not known, and is always a concomitant of matter, hence must be as natural as matter.

If spirit is life, and life is natural, how foolish it is to designate spirit as something supernatural, and how absurd to talk of spirit world or spirit body.

When we talk of natural life and spiritual life, we evolve nonsense.

There is but one life: life and spirit are synonymous.

We have seen that differentia of life manifestations results from differentia of environment, aided primarily by hereditary impress.

Hereditary impress implies and embraces the impress of knowledge acquired by our progenitors.

Environment, together with hereditary impress, accounts for all differentia of types, both physically and mentally.

The inevitable waste of all animates, of all organic bodies, begets discomfort followed by discontent; these in turn arouse desire to repair the waste; success gives joy; joy enhances the will power to do; happiness is thereby increased.

Happiness is the goal all animates strive for, from the lowest to the highest.

CHAPTER III.

HEAT.

WHAT is heat?

Heat is a phenomenon almost as inexplicable as life and matter.

Heat possibly is interblended with both — possibly an inherent attribute of both; consequently may be considered as coexistent with both.

When we consider that the inherent attributes of matter consist of attraction by gravity, attraction of magnetism, attraction by affinity, repulsion by non-affinity, all of which presuppose motion, we must conclude that motion is the normal condition of matter, and is coexistent therewith.

Scientists who have made heat and motion a specialty, state that even in a solid metallic bar there is constant molecular motion, that every atom is polarized.

Now, inasmuch as the positive attracts the negative, and *vice versa*, it follows that the proximity of atoms gives rise to constant change of polarity, which inevitably creates constant motion; the motion, however, is so minute that no sensible heat is developed thereby.

Thus, practically, we have motion without heat.

Heat has never been considered a property of any one of these imponderables that give rise to motion. Motion, however, is a prerequisite to the development and manifestation of heat. It is silly to state that "heat is a mode of motion," inasmuch as motion is only the mode or means whereby heat is manifested.

Heat *per se* is wholly different from motion.

Motion being the normal condition of matter, and as matter exists throughout unlimited space, it follows that matter in motion must meet with resistance, which gives rise to friction and the development of heat by combustion.

Heat results from combustion. Combustion results from friction. Friction results from motion. Motion, as already stated, results from attraction of gravity, of magnetism, of affinity of atoms and repulsion of atoms.

Heat is almost the equivalent of life.

Without heat we can have no manifestations of life.

But we have manifestations of heat without the least perception of life.

An excess of heat destroys life manifestations.

An insufficient degree of heat fails of life manifestations.

But it is not logical — we are not warranted — to infer that life is not ever and always present with matter.

The fish frozen as hard as an icicle, with no life apparent, when properly thawed, manifests animate life in all its fulness.

Thus it is seen that certain degrees of heat favor or destroy life manifestations, but in no sense destroy life.

The requisite degree of heat holds in regard to the production of all phenomena; for example, the chemical action of given proportions of elementary substances produce certain degrees of heat and results, whereas different proportions of the same substances produce wholly different results.

It is well known that all growth of life phenomena results from appropriation and assimilation of elementary properties resident in matter, that a given degree of heat is requisite both for appropriation and assimilation; right here we find the key to the cause of differentia of all life phenomena.

Different degrees of heat furnish and favor the elimination and assimilation of one or more of the elementary constituents of matter rather than of others; consequently, when change of environment occurs, whereby pabulum of one or more of the elementary substances is furnished in larger quantity than others that may exist in the same substance, vegetate and animate organisms inevitably develop in harmony with the differentia of pabulum thus furnished.

It is well known that the components of all vegetates and animates consist of different proportions of the very same substances; hence it follows that a larger supply of one or more elements and a meagre supply of others must inevitably increase and decrease the various tissues of which each are composed, and as a sequence we have large bones and small bones, long hair and no hair, on the same species.

Again, as no two atoms can occupy the same place at the same time and are constantly changing their environment, it follows that no two animates can have exactly the same environment in the same locality; therefore no two are ever found exactly alike.

It is not known positively whether life manifested first in the vegetate or animate form. Neither is it positively known whether marine or terrestrial life manifested first.

In the germ plasm, in which life is first perceived, it is not possible to foretell whether life will eventually develop in vegetate or animate form (Agassiz, Huxley).

The organic origin and development of life vegetate result from the chemical action of light — always accompanied with a moiety of heat — upon matter, whereby the attraction and repulsion of atoms result in motion, thus augmenting heat within the atoms.

Heat, motion and moisture pervading inorganic matter enable life — ever present — to assimilate matter into organic form.

The organic origin and development of life, vegetate and animate, are much the same in mode, the latter only requiring a slightly increased degree of heat; but, as previously stated, the exact stage where life vegetate and life animate separate is unperceived, and is as inexplicable as the existence of either.[1]

---

[1] In China, there is a curiosity known as the vegetable worm, Tung-ch'ung-hsia-ts-ao. It begins life manifestations as a worm, and ends as a plant. The worm lives under ground, and is three or more inches long when at full growth,

Prof. J. B. Schnetzler truly says, "that spontaneous motion is not evidence of life, that motion of protoplasm in the cells of leaves is due to moisture and light, whereby oxygen is made to enter through their walls from the underside. . . . In this case, as in all similar cases, we have heat, motion and growth; these are all the evidences we ever have of vegetable life. . . . But when watching the progress of incubation, the moment we see motion we call it evidence of life. And in this case motion is life, and may be called spontaneous."

The professor's conclusion is illogical, inasmuch as motion is the same in each case. He inevitably infers motion to be life in incubation from a prior knowledge gained by experience that motion in incubation always results in life animate. The only true criterion of life animate is motion from volition.

The degree of heat is an important factor in the development of life in any case.

By the increase of heat during incubation, a Frenchman developed monstrosities in chicks, and yet the eggs of fish may be hatched in ten, fifteen or twenty days by a decreased degree of heat, and all will be normal developments when born.

Now, if life is self-existent from all eternity to all eternity, life may never be called spontaneous.

Neither can the manifestations ever be called spontaneous.

In point of fact and philosophy, there is no spontaneity.

---

at which time a vegetable fungus emerges from the back of the neck and grows upward, six to ten inches, and the roots penetrate and fill the body of the worm. Finally both die, and become dry and hard.

Tartarian travellers tell of a vegetable lamb, found on the salt plains west of the Volga, that grows on a stock about three feet high, which is attached to the navel and has legs distinctly formed, and twines about, bending its head to the herbage for food, and its body is covered with a soft and thick down.

> "Cradled in snow and fanned by Arctic air,
> Shines gentle Barometz; thy golden hair;
> Rooted in earth, each cloven foot descends,
> And round and round her flexile neck she bends;
> Crops the gray coral moss and hoary thyme;
> Or laps with rosy tongue the melting wine,
> Eyes with mute tenderness her distant dam,
> Or seems to bleat — a vegetable lamb." — *Darwin*.

Why not? Because there is not one fact or phenomena ever manifested that is wholly original; all have been undergoing preliminary evolution for æons of ages.

All manifestations of life, whether vegetate or animate, result from the involuntary operations of the inherent forces of matter.

The warring of the elements of matter, manifested by repulsion, no less than their harmony manifested by affinity, results in manifestations of life.

The fish frozen by the involuntary operations of matter, and thawed by the same involuntary operations, results in manifestations of life: and is an apt illustration of the origin of life's manifestation, but by no means an illustration of the origin of life. Therefore, life is never spontaneous.

Life is never begotten by sexual intercourse in any manner whatsoever. Matter is only thereby reduced to a condition favorable to evolve manifestations of life already existing.

Professor Tyndall's experiments going to show that life is never spontaneous, were of little value to science, inasmuch as he only succeeded in reducing matter to a condition in which manifestations of life were impossible. We see matter in that condition all around us.

A Chatauqua expounder of philosophy stated that the "fireball theory of the sun would have to be abandoned; that the ice lens of Professor Metius, if accepted at its real value, would change *ab initio* the existing philosophy of the universe." Whereas, its real value is very small indeed.

There is an axiom of science, that results are always analogous to the cause; in scriptural phrase, everything after its kind.

Therefore, heat can only emanate from a body that contains heat. Heat, like all imponderables, requires matter for expression.

Even if there is no heat *per se* in the rays emanating from the sun, they yet contain the inherent property by and with which heat is evolved when they impinge upon matter.

The only source and origin of heat is combustion.

The only source of combustion is matter.

Heat and light are the same; both originate from, and are manifested through, the same medium.

Light *per se* is a degree of combustion too low to evolve perceptible heat, except when the rays are focused.

The more rapid the combustion, the more intense the heat and light emanating therefrom, and *vice versa*.

Now, if space between the earth's atmosphere and the sun is, according to Professor Secchi, or Sindbad, as dark as Erebus, and eighteen million degrees of temperature below zero, and yet does not affect the inherent potency of the sun's rays in the production of heat, why should they become radically changed when passing through a thin transparent medium thirty-two degrees above zero? That ice does not affect the heat-evolving attribute of the sun's rays while passing through it, is evident from the fact that several degrees of heat are evolved and consumed during the passage; and yet the rays remain as potent to evolve heat after the passage as before.

Again, if space is dark, it is because of a lack of sufficient matter therein to produce combustion wherewith to light it.

When the sun's rays enter the earth's atmosphere, its rarity furnishes but little fuel for combustion, and, as a sequence, but little heat or light is evolved at high altitudes. However, when the rays penetrate the more dense atmosphere near the earth's surface, combustion is greater, and, as a sequence, the evolution of heat and light is greater. We thus infer that Jupiter's surface is warmer than the earth's, consequent upon his greater density of atmosphere, arising from his greater attraction of gravity, in conformity with his greater mass.

The sun's rays are no more potent to the production of heat when the earth is at perihelion than when at aphelion, not even when the rays impinge upon a vertical surface, although nearly three million miles nearer.

With a moderate lens, the writer burnt his hand with rays focused from a small argand oil-burner ten feet distant, with a space temperature of forty degrees Fahrenheit, thus demonstrating that results are analogous to cause.

Combustion never consumes; it only resolves matter into inorganic condition.

Millions of years hence, combustion — by the sun's rays — will have resolved the earth's atmosphere and all atmospheric resources into something inert. Whereupon the earth will give up the ghost. All life manifestations will have departed therefrom.

Life, too, may seek other spheres. Grandma earth will have become a dead moon. Those of her children not evolved sufficiently to abide everywhere will betake themselve to the atmospheres of other planets, and there continue evolution in acquisition of knowledge.

CHAPTER IV.

FUNCTIONAL PHENOMENA.

SENSATION is the first attribute manifested by animation.

Sensation gives rise to desire; desire gives rise to volition.

Sensation, however, originates nothing; it only calls into action latent attributes.

These three attributes are so closely allied as to be almost inseparable; the latter two, however, are dependent for action upon the first.

Motion, heat and growth are all perceived — are all manifested in vegetable, but no sensation whatever.

The sensitive plants (mimosa and guaxillo) shrink when the finger is pointed thereat, consequent upon an electrical or magnetic current thus transmitted from the person. The phenomena is electrical or magnetic; it is not sensational.

Sensation, desire and volition are not originated spontaneously at the moment of manifestation. Each is a result of operations (of a *vis a tergo*) that have required æons of ages preparatory to the consummation thereof.

Sensation begins at the precise stage where animation supersedes vegetation.

Sensation arises from a wasting of the specific organic form; and is immediately joined by desire to maintain the specific form; whence arises volition as executive attribute. Herein we see how closely the three are interrelated, and yet their action is not synchronous.

Function is never a result of design.

Foreordination has no existence.

Function is developed from pre-existent life, united with matter.

Its origin and development result wholly from necessity arising from fortuitous or adverse environment.

Every phenomenon is exactly what antecedent and present environments have made it.

Natural phenomena never manifest design.

Natural phenomena exist only by virtue of necessity, arising from environment, and must inevitably be in harmony with environment, whilst environment is wholly the result of physical forces.

These premises have been entertained by the writer since 1865 — were published in 1867. Therefore it is with much satisfaction that he now learns that the same have been held by the distinguished scientist, Dr. Karl Semper.

Dr. Semper demonstrated most conclusively that change of environment modifies organic forms. He caused *artemia salina* to be transformed into *artemia milhousen* by substituting salt water for brackish water. He again caused *artemia salina* to be changed into *branchipus stagnalis* by substituting fresh water for brackish water.

Hitherto these had been considered distinct species.

These transformations were not effected suddenly, but required several generations. The first struggled for existence under the new conditions required. The second had a lesser struggle, whilst the third generation, having become adapted to the new environment, required only the ordinary effort to maintain existence.

This struggle of adaptation to environment is about all there is, or ever was, of hereditary inheritance.

The only trait of inheritance shown, when change of environment is first met, is the struggle for existence in organic form, without regard to specific form transmitted by ancestry.

Although controverted by distinguished scientists, there is no axiom of science more clearly established than the fact that change of environment works change of specific forms of body and a correlative change of functional organs in harmony therewith.

The grubs in the cells of the working bees are ofttimes changed and developed into queen bees by change of food (A. I. Root).

The change in this case is so great as to constitute almost or altogether a change of sex.

The change is not only one of bodily form, but also of reproductive functions and mind, as evidenced by demeanor of action.

These radical changes all occur by change of food alone, unaided by change of exterior environment.

Now, inasmuch as change of climate always works change of food, differentia of species is easily accounted for.

In this phenomenon we see nature thwarted by design.

Chicks have been hatched that were developed into monstrosities by an increased degree of heat during incubation.

Nature again thwarted by design.

A young tree is projected from the cliff, with roots penetrating a cleft. The roots are only on the side next the cleft. Not from design but from necessity, otherwise the tree would not have existed.

Non-existence precludes design.

Natural selection presumes ability to choose.

Necessity consequent upon peculiar environment precludes choice.

All life phenomena must of necessity maintain their organism by food furnished within their reach, or cease to exist.

Darwin explains natural selection to be the survival of the fittest.

With all his great intellectual grasp, he yet failed to fully comprehend that environment dominated all phenomena.

Environment is nature. But environment begets necessity, instead of selection.

All life phenomena, of both vegetate and animate, result from fortuitous or adverse conditions.[1]

[1] Naturalists of ordinary intelligence inevitably conclude that the myriads of differentiated animates found, especially marine habitants, could only have resulted from hap-hazard environment.

The sower went out to sow. All his seeds were good; but, alas, some fell among thorns and were choked; some fell on stony ground, sprung up and withered; some fell on good ground and survived. Herein we clearly see the survival of the fortuitous only, not the fittest.

The champion of the barnyard struts his brief, brilliant career, and is challenged by a second-rate rooster. The two are so nearly matched that both are well nigh slain in the conflict. Up comes a third-rate cockerel — fresh as the morning — and slays them both; and he, a third-rater, reigns.

A clear survival of the fortuitous.

We have had but one fittest American for President of the United States.

Materialists — always arrogant, but not always logical — assert that the dissolution of an organism renders extinct the life manifested therein.

While maintaining the indestructibility of matter, the correlation and conservation of forces, they yet assert the extinction of life when the body ceases to manifest animation.

Thus denying the law of conservation and wholly ignoring the demonstrable fact that life exerted as will is a force.

Will force, like all imponderable forces, can only manifest through matter; but, unlike all other imponderable forces, can only manifest through matter when coupled with life.

Now, inasmuch as all imponderable forces are invisible, it follows that their manifestations are only distinguishable by peculiar characteristics. Will force alone manifests intelligence.

Intelligence is never suspected of emanating from electric, magnetic or thermal forces.

Intelligence always implies the immediate presence of life.

Will force alone has speech.

The universe is a unit.

Not one atom can be added thereto nor subtracted therefrom.

Life, too, is a unit, that pervades the universe, and may be considered as constituted of an infinite number of attributes.

Under favorable conditions it is capable of manifesting sensational, affectional and intellectual attributes *ad infinitum.*

Matter is constantly being evolved; not in gain of might, not in power, but in its susceptibility to be controlled by mind.

Will power, or force, is always coupled with intelligence.

By will power all intelligence is imparted.

Intelligence is manifested and imparted in many ways and degrees, but is always manifested through matter, and is never mistaken for electricity, magnetism, gravity or heat, or any semblance of these.

Now, then, when during a long period we have become familiar with peculiar and special intelligence, emanating from a special organic form, and when, after many years have passed since the dissolution of the peculiar and familiar organism, we perceive intellectual manifestations expressed through inanimate inorganic objects, the thoughts of which are identical with those we remember, having been previously expressed through the old familiar organism — intelligence by which the old organism is remembered and identified — it is logical to conclude that intelligence survives dissolution of organic forms; and, inasmuch as life is a prerequisite of all intellectual manifestations, it follows that life, too, with mind is present. And thus the law of conservation is vindicated, that life with all its acquired knowledge continues to exist after dissolution of visible organic forms.

This crucial test of identity by special and peculiar intelligence has been verified by millions.

Individuality is never abrogated.

In the lowest organic forms of life, sensation, desire and will are only exerted to procure food, whereby the specific organic body may be maintained.

But, owing to the constant and almost infinite changes that matter has undergone throughout æons of ages, the conditions requisite to existence become so altered that new modes of effort to obtain food requisite for subsistence are inevitable and inexorable; and unless the new conditions are met, the existing organic forms all perish.

Every change in the mode of procuring food adds a new attribute, another degree of will power to execute, which power eventually becomes almost unlimited.

In all forms whereby life is manifested, life as a unit remains the same; manifestations only differ. Immediately upon the dissolution of any specific form of union with matter, life with all its original and acquired attributes is transferred into a new material body, ethereal in substance and invisible to normal vision.

This transition of life from visible to invisible matter is not a supernatural phenomenon.

Ethereal, invisible matter is as natural as gross, visible matter, and is subject to the force of gravity in the exact ratio of its mass, the same as gross matter.

Nor does this transition to a new material body constitute a new life.

It is the same old life existing and manifesting under new conditions.

This adaptation to new conditions has been life's constant work for æons of ages.

Neither is this transition a transfer to a supernatural world or sphere, only to a new sphere of this world.

Life on this planet ever remains subject to mundane laws.

The change only consists in a transition from the visible to the invisible sphere.

Life is ever wholly invisible, even to clairvoyant vision; but this new ethereal body now inhabited, and through which and by which life continues to manifest, is as clearly visible to clairvoyant vision as gross matter is to normal vision.

Clairvoyant vision is sometimes manifested by those who inhabit the gross flesh body, and is possessed at all times by those who inhabit ethereal bodies.

Owing to the almost infinitesimal quantity of matter requisite for the ethereal body, the attraction of gravity exerts but little power thereon, and may be wholly overcome by the fiat of the will.

In the aerial sphere of life there are billions and trillions of human beings who count for little more than flies do here.

In this sphere of life we inhabit great ponderous bodies that must be fed and clothed and sheltered; consequently we crowd and jostle each other much as cattle do when penned. Whereas, in the aerial sphere there is no competition; all are limited to their capacity to devise and execute by will power.

"I go to prepare a place for you" is a saying, like many others imputed to Jesus, that is largely deluding.

Parents in this sphere of life prepare physical comforts for expected offspring, furnish luxurious homes for their children during the whole period of life in the flesh. Whereas, in the higher sphere of life, all inevitably rely upon their own resources, subject only to the tuition of those who are met there. Abundance of gold and luxurious homes, carried over from this sphere in subjective form, stand accredited to the individual possessor; they are not listed on change, are not transferable on the books. Material there, with which to build, is abundant and free, monopolized by none; but is worthless to those who lack the implements of construction. The essentials are honesty, industry and kindness; all else are impedimenta. None can build wisely without the genius of comprehension and execution; these are largely deficient in those for whom luxurious homes have been provided by parents in this sphere. There the mind is everything; intelligence that conduces to goodness shines as pure gold among dross sand.

Oh, get thee wisdom of the kind whose fruit is goodness, that you may in the one eternal day dazzle as an electric light, that in the darkest night attracts myriads of insects from their aimless flight!

Notwithstanding the many beauteous life phenomena so tenderly loved, and around which our hearts ever cling, when we contrast life phenomena with physical phenomena (wherein no life ever manifests), life phenomena dwindle to nothing.

It is like comparing a drop of water with the mighty ocean.

When we behold the unsurpassed grandeur of mountain and

vale, the matchless beauty of fleecy clouds, the bright genial sunshine, the terrific storms of winds and waves, the flood and ebb tide of the abyss of waters, the earth's quake, the volcanoes' throes of molten rivers, the lightnings' flash, the thunders' roll by which earth and firmament tremble, the starry hosts, the ceaseless roll of billions of suns and planets upon their axes and their more magnificent orbital revolutions, — all, all proclaim that matter, by and through its inherent forces, dominates and rules the universe.

The force that governs matter is part of nature.

One dominant phenomenon of nature is motion.

If motion could be abrogated, little or no change of matter could occur.

The constant change in the polarization of atoms necessitates motion; whereby atoms that affiliate, and atoms that repulse, clash together, resulting in an infinite number of diverse conditions and phenomena.

But motion *per se* never begets, nor manifests intelligence or life.

The constant evolution of matter results principally from the inherent forces of matter, namely, attraction and repulsion, giving rise to heat and motion. But life being everywhere present, its affinity for matter has enabled it to manipulate and surcharge matter with life's attributes an infinite number of times during numberless ages.

Gross minds inhabit gross matter.

Cultured minds inhabit matter that has been refined by the potency of mind operating thereon for æons of ages. The only law of nature is progression.

In the examination of geological strata it is seen that all life, vegetate and animate, has been gradually undergoing evolution from a lower to a higher organism.

In some cases, however, we perceive retrogression, owing to adverse environment. But progression is the rule and law.

Mind, we have seen, is an attribute of life animate, and is constantly gaining and accumulating knowledge by experience with matter in its organic form, is constantly gaining more and better control of matter.

And in time, as eternity rolls on, will become master of matter.

Then the universe will be controlled by mind instead of matter.

Then floods and famines will cease to fret us; then cyclones and earthquakes and volcanoes will cease to destroy. The war of elements will be no more. Then harmony of concord will reign supreme.

Then peace and happiness will possess the universe.

CHAPTER V.

MAN.

WHAT is man?

Man is a metaphysical phenomenon.

He is a complex being.

He is a component of life and mind.

His complete make-up consists of intellectual, sensational and affectional attributes expressed through matter.

In point of fact and philosophy, all animates combine and possess the very same components of man.

Notwithstanding man's complexity, he is more amenable to analysis than either life or matter.

Mind in the abstract, in its germ, in its quiescent state, exists without origin, because of its inseparable union with life; yet it had an origin of development. This origin of development began when life became united with matter in organic form. If, however, life and matter have always been united, then mind began to develop (evolve) the moment change of environment occurred, the moment life manifested.

Man has no mental trait that distinguishes him from other animates, except only in degree of excellence. Indeed, man is excelled by other animates in each of the five senses; but, in the whole collectively, he excels all others.

Nor has man anything physically to distinguish him from all other animates, except possibly the small flexor muscle of the thumb, which arose from accident or fortuitous environment.

This slight differentia in anatomy enabled man to do that which he otherwise would have failed to do. It gave him facility to accomplish things that eventually became an educator to his mind.

The mind educated the hand, and in return the hand educated the mind.

This reciprocal aid of each is illustrated by combustion. When a fire is kindled in an open space, the air atoms expand and for want of room ascend upward in a current; the more dense air surrounding is forced in and drawn into this upward current, producing a wind, the oxygen of which feeds the flame.

An increase of flame increases the volume of upward current, and in turn increases the inflow of dense air, whereby each mutually supports and enhances the other.

Thus the mind and hand mutually aid each other to an increase of comprehension and dexterity.

The status of man as at present found, both mentally and physically, has been attained by imperceptible progress throughout unknown ages.

This progression was caused wholly by change of environment, fortuitous or otherwise, aided by mental impress of progenitors.

In view of the constant change in the conditions of matter, differentia of animates is inevitable, both as regards species and varieties of the same species.

Inasmuch as all animates are but an aggregation of atoms of matter dominated by life and mind, and as no two atoms can occupy the same place at the same time, it follows that the environment of every atom is different from that of every other atom; hence the differentia of all animates.

Theologians minus philosophy tell us that man is the only creature that possesses a conscience, whereby he is enabled to distinguish right and wrong; which renders him sensible of his accountability to a superior; that this conscience is a special endowment by a supreme being who is infinite in wisdom.

Now these theological premises would have weight with logicians if they were supported by facts.

But inasmuch as we find that conscience with some people is exactly the opposite of the conscience of others — even in civilized nations, where environments are much the same; whilst in barbarous nations whose origin was the same as civilized people, the same contrariety is found, but less emphasized — thence it follows that conscience is wholly a matter of education; that right and wrong, even as perceived in the abstract, are matters of education; whilst education at all times is wholly a result of environment, over which people have little or no control whatever.

In view of the foregoing facts the conclusion is inevitable that a supreme being perfect in wisdom has had nothing whatever to do with the endowment of man with a conscience that is so amenable to environment.

We further find that all animates susceptible of education have a conscience — the same in kind as man; limited, however, to their degree of knowledge. Organic form, together with environment, determines the degree of knowledge.

We have to descend very low in animate organism to find one not susceptible of education; and when we think we have succeeded, it may be the fault of our own dull perceptions.

Why, the very geese know by the tone of the yell, that they have entered the garden without permission and hasten to get out. Again, I knew a horse that during the night would leave the pasture for the corn-field, and after feeding would return to the pasture, and be found lying asleep in the morning. Cases of this kind are numberless, wherein conscience is as clearly discerned as when man is caught stealing.

The only true definition of conscience is a knowledge of having done that which we think, or know, has been forbidden by those who have power to punish us.

Conscience is a distinct attribute, apart from memory; but its manifestation pre-supposes both memory and knowledge.

We may concede the fact that circumstances ofttimes modify right and wrong, that right under some circumstances would be wrong under different circumstances; and yet there are rights that are always right.

It is always right to appropriate the products of your own labor for your own use, whilst it is always wrong to appropriate for your own use the product of others.

This is an absolute truism, whether relating to civilized or barbarous people.

Now, if a supreme being, perfect in wisdom, had endowed man alone with a conscience, surely all men would have the same conscience under the same circumstances; and yet we have seen that no two have the same conscience under the same environment; also that no two can possibly have the very same environment. But, fatal to the endowment theory, we find that where environments are imperceptibly different, the consciences of individuals are as different as right and wrong in their most glaring aspects; whereas, if the theory be true, the difference should be hardly perceptible.

Again, we are told that man is the only creature endowed with reason, and that reason is likewise a special endowment by a supreme being perfect in wisdom.

This assertion, like the endowment theory of conscience, fails by analysis.

All animates that have memory also have reason.

All animates that lay up food for future use have reason, resulting from memory of the necessity.

Originally there may have been no necessity.

The necessity arose from change of environment.

If the change was great or sudden, all perished; but if the change was such as to make it barely possible for animates to live through adverse seasons, in time the effort required to live would educate them to lay up food in advance for time of need.

This education results from knowledge of the necessity, as remembered.

Prior to the necessity, no knowledge or memory could have existed relative to the necessity; knowledge and memory coupled with necessity culminated in reason.

Education implies imparting and receiving knowledge.

All knowledge is obtained by mental impress.

It matters not how the impress is made. It may be made by voice, by look, by gesture or by invisible, inaudible will power.

The latter is the only mode of imparting knowledge to animates prior to birth.[1]

The fœtus, having a physical connection with the mother, receives therefrom all life forces, surcharged with all the physical and mental qualities of the mother.

During gestation the mother is physically and mentally occupied by all the necessities arising from her peculiar environment, consisting of procuring food and shelter and eluding danger, and thus imparts to the fœtus, physically and mentally, much of her own individuality; consequently, when the fœtus is born, it is already educated to comply with the demands of environment.

The truth of this is .evident, as shown by the many peculiar mental traits and physical markings of offspring, that are clearly traced to some unusual mental shock given to the mother during pregnancy.

A twig broken from a tree and planted, will grow to be a tree like unto the parent from which it was taken, because the environments are the same; its life forces continue to be the same. Not so with the fœtus. Although the connection of the fœtus with the parent is as perfect and full as the twig to the tree, the moment the fœtus is detached from the parent its environment is changed. The life forces and mental impress of the parent continue much the same; but the change of environment is constantly modifying the sum total of all its mental and physical endowments.

Again, as the environment of the mother can never be the very same during each gestation, it follows that offspring of the same parent must differ in mental and physical characteristics.

Therefore, when environment changes, whereby the laying up food for future use ceases to be a necessity, animates accustomed to provide food in advance will continue to store up food for a few generations; but inasmuch as the necessity no

---

[1] It is the stupid and unimpressible who think their own thoughts.

longer exists, the mental impress is not given, and as a sequence, food for future use is no longer stored.

The education of the lower order of animates is limited to one object, of procuring food; as we ascend the scale we find that food and shelter are required. Advancing still higher, food, shelter and raiment are all required, together with amusement and culture added thereto.

Thus it is seen that reason and conscience are each the result of education; that education is the result of mental impress; that mental impress is wholly a result of environment; consequently, differentia of animates always harmonizes with the peculiar environment.

The writer when a boy found a wild turkey sitting on eggs; he put the eggs under a chicken hen; in a few days the eggs all hatched. But, greatly to his surprise, every one showed the wild turkey impress, and struck for the woods and freedom the moment they left the shell. He built a board pen around the hen; but one and all found holes and skedaddled, thereby clearly demonstrating the natural mother's wild[1] impress prior to birth.

Every one after his kind, you know.

Experience proves that if the little turks had been held in captivity under domesticating influences, their progeny in time would have lost their wild mental impress.

To further show that reason is not alone peculiar to man, the writer once owned a horse that knew enough to go under shelter when it rained. He has seen him increase his speed from a trot to a gallop to gain shelter ere the shower caught him.

The writer also saw a Thomas bring two live mice into the door-yard to have a nice play; but Thomas soon discovered that two live mice was one too many to play with at one and the same time. However, being master of the situation, he very deliberately held one mouse down with his paws while he ate the other, and then resumed play.

---

[1] Educational.

Again, the writer owned a dog that had the lamentable misfortune to have both his hind legs cut off with a mowing machine; but he managed to adapt himself to this extreme and sudden change of environment. He would rear his hinder parts up and balance himself like an athlete and walk away on his two fore-legs. This was an adaptation to change of environment by *reason*, wholly independent of parental impress.

CHAPTER VI.

OBJECTIVE AND SUBJECTIVE PHENOMENA.

WITHOUT the objective we could have no subjective phenomena.

Subjective phenomena are objective things perceived by contemplation.

Subjective phenomena are the ideal, or mental, impress of the objective.

The objective is visible to normal vision.

The subjective is invisible to normal vision.

We live in one world, with two spheres — the visible and invisible spheres.

First, we have the gross matter and analogous phenomena; after which we have ethereal sublimated matter with analogous phenomena.

After we have left the visible gross body, and have donned the invisible ethereal body, and have entered the invisible aerial sphere, we find that much of the objective here has become the subjective there; that the subjective there is as clearly perceived as the objective is here.

Notwithstanding we have had millions of communications from those who dwell in the invisible aerial sphere, we still entertain a very dim perception of its constitution and reality.

A thousand descriptions of the aerial sphere, by a thousand different persons dwelling there, must necessarily be different and apparently contradictory, consequent upon the different experiences and impressions each received while in the flesh. Therefore, each eagerly describes and revels in the enjoyment of subjective things that were their chief objects of joy while residents here.

It could not be otherwise; we are ever creatures subjected to and dominated by environment.

Owing to our greatly increased sensibility, upon entrance into the aerial sphere, subjective phenomena become, if possible, more realistic than objective phenomena are here. Flowers, fruits, mountains, vales, lakes and rivers are perceived there only in subjective form; they have no existence in the aerial sphere except in the subjective form as a reflex of the objective.

We enjoy landscape scenery there, as we enjoy mountains and streams in dreams here; but it is more realistic.

On the contrary, however, all animate phenomena in the aerial sphere manifest in objective form; but all physical and vegetable phenomena, being void of mind, fail, in consequence thereof, to give any expression, and are not present except in subjective form as perceived by each animate resident there.

All animate phenomena, whether in this gross visible sphere or resident in the invisible aerial sphere, manifest only through matter in objective form.

Now, notwithstanding all animates in the invisible sphere possess material bodies, yet they are incapable of perceiving subjective phenomena without a prior knowledge of the same in the objective.

Objective phenomena must first be seen by normal vision ere they can be contemplated in the subjective.

The equatorian, who never saw ice in the objective form, is unable to see it in subjective form.

A premature departure from this sphere of life is much to be deplored, inasmuch as it requires many years to fully comprehend and receive a distinct mental impress of objective phenomena, in order that we may have a realistic perception of the same objects when we become residents of the aerial sphere, where all phenomena are subjective, except animate phenomena. In the aerial sphere inanimate phenomena are largely a blank to all who have not become familiar with the objective in this sphere.

Herein we see the beauty and utility of reincarnation. As all knowledge results from mental impress, distinct impressions can only arise from objective phenomena. Therefore, those who depart prematurely can only gain knowledge of objective phenomena by aid of and through matter as viewed through mediumistic animates in the flesh, or by reincarnation.

Thus it is seen that our environments here largely determine our environments there.

When denizens of the aerial sphere manifest to us here in material (objective) form, now known as materializations, each one gives us a clew to their former environment when in the flesh.

The lady of fine culture will clothe her person with silk and satin and bedeck herself with lace and diamonds, while the Indian woman — the child of nature rather than art — clothes herself with a blanket and adorns her person with paint and feathers. "Every one after his kind."

Each gives expression to the mental impress received during life in the flesh.

Thought is immaterial; but it is a phenomenon as real as life, and requires material for inception and expression.

If we did not inhabit material bodies in the aerial sphere, we would be void of all mental impress and power of expression.

The philosophy of reincarnation is not fully comprehended. The logic of evolution leads to reincarnation, and necessitates its application to all animates.

We have seen that change of environment, as a rule, works progression; but it may, under adverse conditions, work retrogression. Reincarnation implies a re-entrance into the same kind of body, or into one analogous to the body inhabited while in the flesh in some former period, whereby the reincarnated animate can more readily gain knowledge of objective phenomena, by which alone all knowledge of subjective phenomena is obtained, and which are the bases of all knowledge.

Reincarnation, unlike change of environment, never works retrogression. The reincarnate may re-enter a lower organism than the one previously occupied, and thus begin evolution anew from a lower plane; and when favored with a fortuitous environment, evolve to a higher plane than previously attained. But, as a rule, reincarnates always re-enter a higher organism than the one previously occupied while in the flesh.

As previously stated, man is constituted of life and mind. Life is a unit. Mind is a component of many attributes emanating from life, embracing the misnamed five physical senses, with perception and memory added.

Scientifically speaking, we have no physical senses. All our senses, so called, are mental senses.

It is not our eyes that see or our ears that hear. We only see and hear with and through our eyes and ears.

All our sensibilities are wholly mental, evolved from the organic connection of life with matter, whereby expression is possible and wherein sensibility alone originates.

When bereft of our flesh body, all our so-called five senses remain intact, and accompany us wheresoever we go, forever.

CHAPTER VII.

"WHO BY SEARCHING CAN FIND GOD?"

MAN in his lowest, crudest state accepted all natural phenomena as a matter of course, never questioning from whence any phenomena came.

Eventually he evolved to a higher degree of knowledge; then he inquired how and whence came natural phenomena; and being capable himself of making some things, he imagined that superior beings made all those things he saw but was unable to make.

Those superior beings eventually became what are now called gods. He had a special god for each phenomenon. He imagined a god of the ocean, a god of the mountains; of the plains, of the storms, a god who made the thunder and rain.

Each conjectured a god after his own imagery.

When man had further progressed in a knowledge of natural phenomena, he struggled to get a closer view and better idea of the gods.

Heraclitus conjectured that fire was the source of all phenomena. Thales taught that water was the source; Ananagores, air; Democritus, atoms; Epicurus, matter and space; Plato, mind and matter. Each, however, failed to define the origin of their creative elements, which implies that each inferred the self-existence of their creative sources.

In this year of our reckoning, with our present knowledge of natural phenomena, we are enabled to give a clearer definition of the cause of phenomena.

Names ofttimes are things; for example, the color blue is

blue, only because it is called blue. So, too, with the term God; God is just what each one makes him.

Thence, if we must have a god, let us try and have a god that is logically in harmony with phenomena, a god that can be recognized by one or more of the attributes by which all our knowledge is obtained.

Thus, What is the creative source of phenomena? In short, What is God?

God is spirit.

What is spirit?

Spirit is life.

What is life?

Life is that which manifests germination, animation and mind in matter.

What is germination?

Germination is a manifestation of life in matter, resulting in growth of specific form.

What is animation?

Animation is a manifestation of life in matter, resulting in growth, whereby intelligence is evolved and manifested.

Thus God is perceived, is found all around; wherever life vegetate, or life animate, is found, there God is, there God dwells.

Thence life is God, and God is life. And life is ubiquitous, is unchangeable from everlasting to everlasting, blessed and only blessed evermore.

Heat, light, electricity, solar and terrestrial magnetism are each wholly invisible to normal vision; each, however, is intelligibly recognized by its peculiar but mute expression through matter, and gives rise to no controversy about its existence. Therefore, inasmuch as the manifestations of life are so visibly present in all vegetation, in all animation, God therein becomes as realistic as matter.

Why search farther? Have we not found Him?

CHAPTER VIII.

HYPERBOLE METAPHYSICAL.

"I and my Father are one."
"I am in the Father and the Father is in me."
"Why sayest thou, Show me the Father?"
"He that hath seen me hath seen the Father."

The above sayings imputed to Jesus are certainly very presumptuous, containing only a germ of truth.

Hegel, the great metaphysician, says that in all cases the truth of one proposition implies the falsehood of all opposite propositions.

We will try and extract the germ of truth from these several misapprehensions.

It is quite possible that Jesus himself did not apprehend the full import of these sayings. However, he spoke on a level with the plane of intelligence of his day, when man was considered as constituted principally of flesh, bones and blood.

This view may shock the sensibilities of many who never dream that others have sensibilities equally as tender and yet have the courage of their convictions. True, we read of the marvellous wisdom manifested by Jesus at the age of twelve years when found in the temple in the midst of the doctors, answering and asking questions; all of which was accounted as veritable evidence of his godship. Whereas the writer was well acquainted with a little darling of three summers, who greatly surprised her mother while walking the streets of a large city, by reading the sign-boards on the houses, having never been taught her letters; but no one ever imputed divinity to this dear child. Yet, verily, a little goddess she was, and left earth for heaven many years before she arrived at the age of thirty-three. However, to return to our subject, we may state that the Father and Son are *one* to the extent that both are constituted of life and mind.

The attributes of mind in the Father, however, are latent; while with the Son they are active.

The attributes of mind can only become active by and through organic union of life with matter; and the moment life obtains this union, life and mind become individualized. One (or more) of the attributes of mind becomes active, is allied with the organic individual, and thereby ceases to be *one* with the Father; yet inasmuch as the Father is life, together with mind in its *latent* state, while the Son is life together with mind in its *active* state, consequent upon the Son's organic union with matter, it is thus seen that the Father and Son are one in a limited degree. It is also seen how it is, and to what extent, the Father is in the Son and the Son in the Father; life *per se* is the same in each.

The declaration, "He that hath seen me hath seen the Father" is one of much latitude, and was made under a misapprehension or false assumption.

In a strict sense, it is very certain that no man hath seen the Father (life) "at any time."

Hence, if the Father and Son are one, it follows that no man hath seen the Son. Man truly is as invisible as God, is in the image of God.

God is *life* embodying all the latent elements of intelligence. Man is life embodying all the active elements of intelligence. Life and intelligence are immaterial; consequently they are wholly invisible.

If we should concede the literal truth of the sayings, " I and the Father are one," " He that hath seen me hath seen the Father also," and that the Son has been seen, it follows that in the personality of the Son we have a tangible something whereby we may obtain some valuable knowledge of the impersonal Father.

Is not this a fair and logical proposition?

Throughout the history of man it has not been infrequent for man to assume that he was God, even while in the flesh, while great numbers of men have been deified by men after departure.

Our analysis of Jesus must be drawn wholly from the New Testament.

The life of Jesus by modern authors is largely imaginary.

In the New Testament we read that Jesus the Son hungered, thirsted, wearied, slumbered, sorrowed, and in all things was subject to like passions as other men.

None of these, however, ever occurred to the Father. Why not? Because the instant He (life) became united with matter He became personal and ceased to be the Father.

Jesus said that all his power to do miraculous work came from above.

Not from the Father. Why should it, if he and the Father were one? Yet elsewhere we have shown that all power of intelligence does emanate from life, the Father.

Again, we read that Jesus' power to work miracles was limited. Not because the efficacy of the power was limited, but because of adverse environments he was not always able to avail himself of the power; consequently he failed as other men.

He told his disciples that they had, or could have, the same power from above, and, indeed, might excel him in miraculous works.

Throughout the Scriptures we find but few, if any, miracles wrought by Jesus that were not duplicated by other men.

Elijah, Elisha and Paul all brought the dead to life. All the apostles — yea, and thousands of others since their day, and in our day — have worked the same kind of miracles that Jesus wrought.

From all of which we learn that Jesus was emphatically a man much the same as other men; that he was the son of Joseph and Mary; brother of James, of Joses, of Simon and

Judas; was a carpenter by trade; toiled daily with his father for a number of years, same as other boys.

It is claimed that Jesus stilled the waves. But did he? Stilling the waves involves too much power for billions of men even at this day. There is no power at present in existence to still the ocean waves; they are stilled only by the winds working out their own equilibrium.

Jesus positively disclaims any special power not common to other men; in fact, Jesus was only a man begotten and born same as other babies.

I have this direct from his mother. Why not? She knows all about it.

None but deluded idiots ever dreamed otherwise.

Thus throughout the analysis of Jesus, the Father as man has eluded us; but the Father as life, the source of all animation, is discovered in all and over all, blessed forever.

If anything further was needed to identify Jesus as a man and only a man, when in the flesh, we might add that when we follow and find him in the aerial sphere, he there possesses the etherial body common to all men who are residents of the aerial sphere.

We find him, not sitting on the right hand of God the Father; we see no Father; we see no throne; but we do see Jesus, and Mary his mother, and Joseph his father, and all his brethren.

CHAPTER IX.

"TO THE UNKNOWN GOD, WHOM YE IGNORANTLY WORSHIP."

WHEN a boy of ten, nobody could tell anything about God I did not already know.

I knew him better than I did my grandfather.

God was a huge, big man, with three heads; and yet he was the father of only one boy.

Besides God, there was another fellow I knew all about. He, too, was a huge, big fellow. He was called the Devil. He was a terrible fellow; he had horns, a split foot, and a tail with a spear on the end.

Neither I nor anybody else had ever seen either; but I had seen pictures of the fellow with horns: that was sufficient. He with the horns was father of us all — just millions of us. Every one of us was born an heir of hell; hell was a pit without a bottom, and yet was full of fire and brimstone.

In my innocence, I was sorely puzzled to know why the Devil had millions of children, and God only one boy and no girl.

I thought how much nicer it would have been if the Devil could have had only one boy, and God have had all the millions of boys, and all the dear girls, too. Ah, me! how I worried over the sad mistake.

For thirty-five years I was hedged around with this Devil and his hell of fire and brimstone, and an angry God that let the Devil have his own way every time. But, thanks to the fortuitous environment of a later day, the angry old God and wheedling old Devil of my childhood and youth have both vanished, and I breathe free as air. Hallelujah! Amen, A-M-E-N!

Idiots talk, and even boast, of the harmony of religion and science; whereas, there is not an atom of science in religion, nor one atom of religion in science. Science is based wholly on facts. Religion is based wholly on imagination.

CHAPTER X.

"THE FATHER IS GREATER THAN I."

The truth of this declaration imputed to Jesus goes without the saying.

Life (the Father) permeates all that manifests life throughout the universe, and possibly every atom of matter in the universe; while Jesus permeates only a few atoms of matter.

As the collective universe is greater than a clod in the valley, even so is the Father greater than Jesus.

Life ever and always represents God the Father, wherever manifested. Therefore when we read that Jesus was God manifested in the flesh, in matter, it is not true — only to the extent that he manifested life, and life is God.

But inasmuch as Jesus does not manifest life in its entirety, he fails to manifest God in his entirety. Moreover, the assertion is equally applicable to all men — to all animates and to all vegetates, the growing sycamore as well as man.

The Father is manifested in all matter that manifests life; whereas Jesus is a manifestation of life and mind through a few atoms of matter, and is restricted to a single organism.

The Father's representation is infinite.

The Son's representation is finite.

Without the Father, the Son could not have existed.

Now, as life is the source whence all intelligence originates, and as life is manifested in vegetation, from whence intelligence is never manifested, and as animation is a prerequisite to the manifestation of any intelligence, it follows that life *per se* is not animate. It is thus seen why animation and mind are the distinctive characteristics of Jesus from the Father.

The originator is greater than the thing originated.

The Son was in the Father, else could not have proceeded from the Father.

The Son was one with the Father until a specific organic union of life with matter occurred, whence animation manifested, whereby the Son became an individuality, a personality.

Life the Father is impersonal.

Life and matter — *pater* and *mater* — being infinite in duration, it follows that the Son animate and all animates are infinite in duration; hence *pater* and *mater* are in all and over all, and are worthy of all homage.

CHAPTER XI.

TRUE AND SPURIOUS GODS.

THREE attributes are requisite to constitute the true God.

He must be ubiquitous, unchangeable and wholly beneficent.

Not an atom of anger, revenge, remorse or hate can ever enter into the component of the true God.

Hitherto all gods have been modelled like unto the modeller; all have been a transcript of the maker's imagination. No man ever did, or ever can, get away from himself. His every act and expression is but a reflex of himself — of what he has seen, heard or felt.

All thought originates from a suggestion of nature, either animate or inanimate.

All must come to him who is within from that which is exterior.

Nothing is original with man; all comes to him secondhanded. Hence, all his gods are the same in divine or diabolic character as the one who portrays them.

Divine or diabolic impressions are given only to those who have a special trend of mind for one or the other.

The more dense the ignorance of the individual or nation, the more numerous and monstrous their gods be.

The more intelligent the individual or nation, the less numerous and more lovable their gods be.

Some people have thousands of gods; some have three gods in one; some have one god only; and some have none.

When man is in his nomadic state, his gods are numerous; all are powerful, tyrannical and bloodthirsty, in harmony with his own being.

When man is cultured, all his gods are beneficent and lovable.

Hence, to reflecting minds it seems strange that while art and science of all kinds, shades and degrees have gradually improved under the impulse of increased knowledge, yet the majority of D.D.'s, LL.D.'s, and Ph.D.'s worship the same old gods of yore, whose make up was conceived when man was totally ignorant of all art and science.

The reaping-hook has been displaced by the horse-reaper and binder, the forked stick by the steel plow, the ox wagon by the steam locomotive, the horse express by the lightning messenger, the raiment of skins by silk and fine linen, the tents of Abraham by Windsor Palaces, and yet the old gods, with all their hideous and cruel attributes, still dominate all nations, savage or civilized, alike.

The contemplation is full of sadness. The legitimate fruit of such worship has drenched the world with human blood.

Oh, that man would learn that the true God is life, that life is God.

Hence He is in all, over all, blessed evermore.

Verily, giving does not impoverish our God, nor withholding enrich him.

The writer has just finished a review of the history of Christianity, and in view thereof is forced to conclude, that if a book, like a tree, is known by its fruit, then the Old and New Testaments are by far the worst books ever published. Their teachings as interpreted by their expounders have, directly and indirectly, caused the most cruel death of hundreds of thousands of human beings.

The Bible would have been no worse, except in quantity, than "Sindbad," had not deity been claimed for its author.

Between the years of 1599 and 1680, 3,400 women were burned in Scotland. During the same period 1,500 were burned in Geneva. In Lorraine, 1,900 were burned. In two centuries 200,000 were slain in some manner as witches.

It is estimated that since Abraham's time, up to the present, the teaching of the Bible has instigated, directly and indirectly, the slaughter of 12,000,000 human beings. Some historians estimate it 70,559,000.[1]

The incentive to murder is threefold. Those who believe, those who disbelieve, and those who differ in belief are each in turn put to death by the faction in power. Most painful to state, the slaughter has not yet ceased : for example, Stanley and others in Africa.

Nothing so heinous is chargeable to any other publications.

Making full allowance for all the good found therein, still the bad submerges all beyond line or plummet.

The Bible inculcates everything that is vile and cruel; the New Testament inculcates fraud from the first to the last line.

The burden of the whole is eternal damnation to all, resulting from Adam's imaginary fall; redemption therefrom only by belief in the saving virtue arising from the lamentable murder of a brother man.

These two beliefs are the substratum and crown of all iniquity.

So long as it is preached that eternal damnation is an inheritance and that redemption therefrom can only come by *vicari*, whether the *vicarius* be a half-skekel, a scapegoat, or the murder of a brother, so long will rapine and murder remain rampant throughout the world.

Anathema Maranatha let all such teaching be.

They who believe in vicarious settlement for sin, never have, and never will cease to sin — never, *never*, NEVER !

---

[1] Killed under Pope Julian, 200,000; by the French massacre, 100,000; by wars on the Waldenses, 150,000; by wars on the Albigenses, 150,000; by Jesuit mobs and tortures, 900,000; by Duke of Alba's orders, 136,000; by tortures of Inquisition, 150,000; by the Irish massacre, 150,000; by wars on Moors of Spain, 1,500,000; by wars on Jews in Europe, 2,100,000 ; in Mexico, South America and Cuba, 15,000,000 ; under bloody Queen Mary, 23,000 ; in East Indies, Europe and America, 50,000,000. Total loss of human lives, as found in authentic history, by papal tyranny, 70,559,000.

CHAPTER XII.

"I AM THE RESURRECTION AND THE LIFE."

THE above saying is one of many imputed to Jesus that contains a germ of truth and an immense amount of misapprehension.

Heretofore we have shown that Jesus is a component of life, matter and mind; that matter is but incidental to manifestations of life and mind; that this combination is common to all men and, indeed, to all animates; that the only characteristic that gives individuality to men is special quality of mind.

When Dr. Watts exclaimed, "'Tis the mind that makes the man," he uttered a truism never to be controverted.

Yes, 'tis the mind that makes man differ from the ox and the ass.

Jesus manifested his own peculiar moiety of mind; the ox and ass do the same.

In no possible construction of the phenomenon life, is, or was, Jesus the resurrection or the life.

This declaration — if correctly rendered — discloses dense ignorance of the phenomenon life and the phenomenon miscalled death.

We now know that life never dies, only ceases to manifest to normal perception; that all the varied attributes of mind that proceed from life never die.

Webster's definition of resurrection presupposes the death of life; it was given under the impression that life, with all its varied attributes, was susceptible of death and was buried with the gross matter through which all had manifested.

No error could be more misleading, inasmuch as man *per se*

is immaterial. How impossible to bury immateriality! No burial precludes resurrection, as defined by Webster and believed by orthodoxy.

We may say with propriety that no man hath life, that no creature hath life. Man *is* life.

"I am the resurrection and the life"; in other words, I am life resurrected, as ye see manifested in me now; that is, I am life animate, not life inanimate.

Life in a grain of wheat is quiescent, is unperceived until resurrected by heat and moisture.

Life in an egg is quiescent, is unperceived until resurrected, until animated by heat and moisture; even so have I been resurrected, have been animated. Consequently, I manifest life resurrected; I am life resurrected. All animates represent life resurrected.

And yet, again, in a strict, logical sense, both in fact and philosophy, Jesus is not life; he only manifests life. No man is life, no creature is life. God the Father is life. He is always *the life*. He permeates all matter. He alone is the life, before as well as after resurrection.

He is the life, whether manifested in fauna or flora.

Creatures have no specific existence whereby they can be distinguished apart from God, apart from life until life has been animated.

Jesus became a son, a creature, the moment life became animated, the moment specific characteristics of life were manifested, prior to which he had no individual existence apart from the Father.

Yes, 'tis only special characteristics that distinguish man from the ass. That is why it is so easy for some men to bray.

It has been said that truth lies at the bottom of the well; and if so, to get there we must descend from the top.

In the philosophic solution of all phenomena we must begin with the apparent on top, and delve downward to basic principles.

Elsewhere we have stated that man was constituted of life, matter and mind. As we progressed in our investigations, we learned that matter was but a prerequisite to manifestation of life and mind, and was not an essential part of man. We also learned that life animate was a prerequisite to manifestation of mind, and was a common but absolute prerequisite of all animates prior to manifestation of mind. Herein we again see that man is not life *per se*, that God alone is life *per se*, that Jesus is not God, that he only manifests God (life) in flesh. All animates do the same.

Speciality of mind gives special form to the material body of all animates.

Now, as life animate is the source whence all intelligence emanates, and as life is manifested in vegetation, in germination whence intelligence is never manifested, it follows that life *per se* is not animate, is not intelligent; else trees might talk. It is thus seen why a specific quality of mind is the only distinctive characteristic of Jesus and, indeed, of all animates from life, the father of all.

It may be objected, that to distinguish the manifestations of life from life *per se* is inconsequential. But unless we get down to basic principles and basic facts, we fail to obtain a clear perception of either God or man; unless we view life as something distinctive from the manifestations of life, our perceptions of life — of God — become dimmed or wholly erased by the manifestations.

We perceive man through the manifestation of life, but lose sight of God in the manifestations that proclaim man.

Having learned that the sun neither rises nor sets, we yet may talk understandingly of phenomena that apparently result from the apparent rising and setting of the sun; otherwise, not knowing the facts, we should be wholly deluded. So, too, with the phenomena of life and man; we must entertain a clear perception of both ere we can have a clear understanding of either.

CHAPTER XIII.

AN IMAGINARY GOD AND SOME OF HIS EXPLOITS.

We read in the Scriptures that "God is love," that "God is slow to wrath and abundant in mercy," "For our God is a consuming fire," "The name of the Lord cometh from far, burning with anger," "His lips are full of indignation," "His tongue is a devouring fire."

The above quotations are the most incongruous and preposterous imaginable.

Their reconciliation or substantiation is wholly impossible.

But if we accept life as God, the first quotation becomes intelligible. Inasmuch as all animates love life, love and life become correlative or convertible terms, thence we may relegate the fire and anger attributes assigned to God out of existence.

To the meek fraud Moses, more than to all others, the Jew and Gentile nations are indebted for the infamous conception of an angry God.

This lamentable misapprehension of God has drenched the world with human blood and filled it with shrieks of woe.

Millions of human beings, including women and babes, have been put to death to appease the imaginary anger of an imaginary God.

Oh, that mine eyes could weep rivers to wash away the blood stains of the slaughtered innocents!

When we reflect, that, even in modern times, the Spanish inquisition, the slaughter of Bartholomew, the hundred thousand Paulicians slain by the Princess Theodora, were all for religious belief, we only gain a faint idea of the vastness of the crime of the infamous conception of an angry God.

Historians tell us that on our own fair continent the ancient Aztecs had 46,000 temples builded to an unknown God, the dedication of each requiring 40,000 human sacrifices.

In Yucatan hundreds of temples are found in ruins, wherein human sacrifices were offered to an angry God.

India teems with sacrificial altars whereon human beings were slain to appease the imaginary wrath of an imaginary God.

Millions of human beings and rivers of blood shed as a propitiation for an imaginary disobedience to an imaginary God!

In justification of this monstrous slaughter of man by man, it is claimed in the Scriptures that this God of Moses has slain billions for the same reason where man has slain only thousands.

Throughout the Scriptures we are assured that long life in the flesh is a blessing much to be desired; we know by experience that this is true. Long existence in the flesh gives experience; experience gives knowledge. Viewed in all its aspects knowledge is the principal factor that makes for happiness.

Now, inasmuch as man and all animates desire to exist in the flesh because such existence gives pleasure, and as happiness is the sole desire of all animates, and as this love of life in the flesh is an inherent element of life, it does seem logical that a being who could create a world and the animates thereof — as Moses tells — with an unquenchable love of existence in the flesh; that such a being, infinite in wisdom and power, would have so arranged that life in the flesh would be prolonged many centuries instead of being cut asunder in the morning of existence.

Why, the very bears rush to the rescue of progeny, risk their own love of life in the flesh for the love of offspring. But, on the contrary, Moses' God remorselessly destroys all.

Moses tells of a deluge — not long since — whereby his God destroyed the animates of the whole earth, good, bad, and indifferent, all alike, except a few of his choice.

In view of the billions of human beings destroyed by physical phenomena wherein man could have no agency, it is monstrous to conceive of a being infinite in wisdom, power and love as the author.

Thirty-one years before the birth of Jesus, Judæa was destroyed by an earthquake whereby 10,000 people were destroyed. Sixteen years after the departure of Jesus, 12,000 perished by an earthquake. Sixty-three years thereafter, Pompeii and Herculaneum were destroyed by an earthquake, and thousands thus perished; and in sixteen years after, these cities were submerged by an eruption of Vesuvius. In the year 526, 250,000 perished by an earthquake. On November 26, 1876, Calcutta was destroyed by a cyclone; 250,000 perished. In 1878, 13,000,000 human beings — whom God's only Son died to save — perished by famine in China.

The love of existence in the flesh is unquenchable in all; and yet this unquenchable love bestowed by this God of infinite love destroys all — if he reigns at all.

Theologians and many others extol beyond stint their imaginary God for the assumed perfect harmony and equilibrium of the universe.

They ignorantly and arrogantly tell us, that every star and planet has been weighed and poised in its appointed place in obedience to law and divine wisdom; whereas the very reverse is true. We find stars huddled together hurly burly; while others are trillions of miles distant from all others.

Nature is absolutely void of harmony throughout. All her operations manifest a constant warfare.

Floods, dearths, famines, pestilence, earthquakes and cyclones, with all their dire results, are increasing in frequency and severity.

The only harmony known in nature is the harmony of discord.

As in music, a great number of discords produce concord.

The subtle elementary substances of matter in gaseous form ever strive to attain an equilibrium; but owing to their elasticity, in obedience to irrevocable forces inherent in matter, they never succeed in establishing an equilibrium that results in harmony.

An illustration is seen in atmospheric motion; for example, owing to the globular shape of the earth and her diurnal rotation, together with undulating and diversified surface, solar heat radiated from the earth's surface is unequal from the whole surface, whereby the equilibrium of the whole atmosphere is destroyed, or rather can never be established, resulting in perpetual atmospheric motion.

It is needless to state that this striving for an atmospheric equilibrium which is never attained is the cause of all floods, famines and cyclones by which billions of human beings have been and are annually destroyed.

"Who removeth mountains, and they know it not."

"Who shaketh the earth out of her place, and the pillars thereof tremble."

"Who commandeth the sun, and it riseth not; and sealeth up the stars."

"Who alone spreadeth out the heavens and treadeth upon the waves of the ocean."

"Lo, he goeth by me, and I perceive him not."

"He passeth by me, and I see him not."

No one who ever lived in the flesh, or may ever live therein, could or would lift their hands and eyes higher than I in adoration of such an exalted being, if such there be.

But inasmuch as no such being has ever been perceived, we forbear to adore.

All the above is, at most, only beautiful imagery.

"Lo, he goeth by me, and I perceive him not."

"He passeth by me, and I see him not."

Thus the whole is given away twice in two lines.

The folk-lore of the South Pacific islanders has no divinity, no devil.

All traditions of ancestry end happily.

No convictions of sin; never heard that "in Adam's fall we sinned all." Happy, happy people!

No fear of hell. No fear of God or Devil.

Are wiser than our scientific materialists.

Do not believe that death, so called, ends all; but, on the contrary, believe that each and all continue to live in the future, in the unseen, invisible world, much the same as here, "with the great gain that yams there are abundant without labor" (Porter).

Four hundred years ago this continent was inhabited by a people, honest, industrious, peaceable, intelligent, hospitable, noble, happy and free.

Although not highly cultured in philosophy and fine arts, they yet had a truer conception of God and the future than the orthodox white man.

They believed, and still believe, in a great Good Spirit — father and friend of all, and enemy of none; believe in an endless life, in an endless happy hunting-ground.

But, alas, the white man came — the white man of fine culture and Christian ethics; came surcharged with a divine miscellany of war, drunkenness, disease, slavery, an angry God and a malignant Devil.

For four hundred years the white man has preached hell and practised damnation toward the aborigines of this land in their most dire form.

For four hundred years the wails of the red man and his women and children have been heard, and have echoed in hill and dale from the Atlantic to the Pacific oceans; and the old infamy is still on.

January, 1891, we read that "twenty-five women and children lay dead in front of the white man's guns."[1]

Thus we find the white man's Christian civilization and slaughter — inseparable — are still as rampant in America as on the dark continent.

Alas, my red and black brothers and sisters, thou, too, art children of the same *pater* and *mater* of us all.

Does culture pay?

Yes, culture pays; but it ought to pay without detriment. The sensibility of the cultured is much more exquisite. They

---

[1] Military report.

enjoy pleasure with greater zest, and suffer pain with greater agony, than the nomad.

But if our pleasures and pains are equal, where is the gain?

Ah! but intelligent culture on the humane plane increases pleasure and decreases pain.

A belief in eternal damnation or a vicarium is not a pre-requisite to fine culture; but, on the contrary, it is a relic of barbarity.

If we could be wholly freed from the fear of an imaginary hell, from an imaginary Devil, from an imaginary God "whose anger is a consuming fire when kindled but a little," how lovely the whole of life in the flesh would be!

The bliss of love; the beauty of flowers and fruits, of mountains and vales, of music and poetry, of paintings, of clouds and sunshine — all these endless, contemplation endless, life endless — how glorious!

On all the isles of the sea, wherever Christianity has been introduced, native population has decreased and licentiousness has increased. And why?

Because the creed of Christianity is, "that all sins may be forgiven."

No greater bounty to sin could be offered.

Our National Government only pays two cents a pound bounty on sugar; and yet there are millions in it.

Whether the decrease of native population and the increase of licentiousness are chargeable to Christianity or its concomitants, the result is all the same; and the crime against humanity is all the same.[1]

Bishop Taylor states, that on the continent of Africa the annual increase of population, over and above those who are claimed to be converted to Christianity, is about 11,000,000; consequently the gospel of salvation by vicarious atonement can

---

[1] "Archbishop Jeffrey, who lived thirty years in India, says that English drinking practices have made a thousand drunkards to one native converted to Christianity by missionary labor. Japan and Persia are also yielding to the drink demon. In Africa the story is the same; the native tribes are steadily disappearing." — *Christian Union.*

never be preached to reach and save the unborn billions. Therefore, the only practical plan for the good bishop to pursue is to slay the millions, and thus save from hell the unborn billions.

This plan is not original with the writer.

Holy Moses tells us that once upon a time God discovered that man's wickedness over the whole earth was so great as to admit but one remedy; notwithstanding God's sons had taken unto themselves wives of the daughters of men — a sorry attempt to improve the breed. Therefore God determined to, and did, destroy the whole race, except a few choice specimens, with which to begin anew, and thus forestall the future necessity of destroying the billions that might thereafter be born.

When great conflagrations rage in cities, beyond control, many houses not on fire are blown up or down to stay the flames, and thus save the city.

CHAPTER XIV.

"HE IS FREE, WHOM THE TRUTH HATH MADE FREE."

TRUTH is fact, and implies a knowledge of facts relative to phenomena.

The false and the true — with locked arms — have travelled together ever since man has been capable of entertaining an idea.

The misapprehension of what constituted man has led him into endless trouble, culminating in the belief and fear of endless torment.

Viewing man as constituted of three elements — life, matter and mind, one part material and two parts immaterial — we learn that he is only an animate of the highest intellectual attainments; that his moral sensibility and standard is wholly a result of fortuitous or unfortuitous education, embodying experiences remembered; that the greater the wisdom thus acquired, the finer and greater the moral capacity and sensibility.

Hence his standard of morality is the result of his knowledge, gained by his experience, and by which he is governed.

All animates desire and seek happiness.

Happiness is the inspiration of all moral sensibility. Moral sensibility is a sense of doing right or wrong, which, as previously shown, is an attribute of all animates.

All animates eventually and inevitably remember acts that contribute to happiness, also those acts that contribute to misery. Consequently, in time, they learn to practise that which gives happiness, and to avoid doing that which gives misery; and just in proportion as they practise doing that which conduces to happiness and cease to do that which conduces to misery, so far are they made "free by the truth."

This is all there ever was or ever will be, of being "made free by the truth." Thus we find that — contrary to M. Arnold's bungling metaphysical philosophy — the desire of happiness is *the something within*, not without, ourselves that eventually makes for righteousness.

CHAPTER XV.

ALL ANIMATES ORIGINATE FROM EGGS.

SCIENTISTS tell us that all animates proceed from eggs; that all eggs in their primordial stage of incubation are the very same in material composition, and give no clew going to show whether the future development will result in a biped, quadruped or reptile; that the future specific development arises from an invisible, imperceptible impress originally given the egg by parentage.

Thus clearly demonstrating the close and exact relation of all animates to the same antecedent law of mental impress and special environment.

The term organic life implies the existence of inorganic life; but inasmuch as inorganic life fails to give expression of its presence, its existence remains unproven.

Life has never been perceived except by and through organic environment.

Now, although in the primordial stage all animates are indistinguishable, yet when once switched off on a new trend of development, they may become and remain new and distinct species until a change of environment again works differentia.

It is the change of individuals by environment that always begets new species; and notwithstanding the change in the individual may be so great as to be denominated a new species, yet each individual retains its own specific entity by reason of the fact that the environment of no two can be exactly the same.

If two atoms of matter cannot occupy the same place at the same time, how impossible it is for two organic beings to have the same environment!

CHAPTER XVI.

TRANCE PHENOMENON.

NOTWITHSTANDING the tenacity with which individuality is held throughout time and eternity, we yet have that most wondrous phenomenon called and known as trance; wherein one or more persons temporarily exchange with, or take possession of, the material body of another.

This exchange is sometimes by mutual consent, and sometimes by force without consent.

Dr. Jerome Kidder, in his work entitled "Plurality of Personality," gives an account of a well-authenticated case of a young lady whose body became somnolent, or entranced, and when aroused, the body was found to be occupied by an entire stranger, one wholly oblivious of all knowledge as previously manifested through this same body.

The former occupant was intelligent, whereas the new occupant manifested childhood knowledge in an adult body.

After this child personality had held possession several months, during which time she had made considerable progress in knowledge, the body again went into the trance condition; and when awaked, lo! the original owner had regained possession, and immediately manifested a remembrance of all her old friends, recommenced life in the flesh just where she had quit in the old body. She had not the faintest idea that she had ever left the old body or that another had ever inhabited the same body.

This alternate occupancy of the same body occurred several times, and continued through several years.

When the second person took possession the second time,

she, too, recommenced the acquisition of knowledge just where she had last quitted the body. She, too, manifested no knowledge that another had ever occupied the same body, or that she had ever been absent from the body.

This incident was not a *double personality;* but, on the contrary, it was two distinct personalities.

The exchange may have been mutual, or otherwise; it may have been an inter-exchange. It was almost or altogether equivalent to a reincarnation.

Life being a prerequisite of knowledge, it is herein demonstrated that both life and knowledge are continuous, inasmuch as the same knowledge and trend of thought were taken up and manifested upon the return of each to the material body.

This trance phenomenon is but little understood by many of the M.D.'s, and Ph.D.'s and nearly all the D.D.'s and LL.D.'s.

Many doctors and scientists consider trance to be only a form of hysteria or catalepsy. Many others believe trance to be the work of the Holy (or unholy) Ghost.

But the trance proper is wholly different from hysteria or catalepsy. Trance consists of one person, out of the flesh body, getting possession of the flesh body belonging to and occupied by another; that is, the immaterial components of man — life and mind — while out of the flesh body, dispossess the immaterial components of man in the flesh, and hold and control the body thus obtained for his or her own use.

When we consider the similitude of many persons as manifested through the flesh, it is not so very strange that an inter-exchange or dispossession of bodies does occur.

While it may be true that an inter-exchange of flesh bodies may occur between individuals yet in the flesh, it is a demonstrated occurrence that persons out of the flesh do frequently gain possession of the body of one yet in the flesh.

The person thus dispossessed requires a habitation also, and thereupon immediately clothes itself with an ethereal material body for its temporary habitation, until it can regain its own flesh body.

This temporary ethereal body is essentially the same as the body we all shall inhabit after we have finally departed life in the flesh.

In the year 1861 when a resident of New York City, the writer made a professional call on a lady who was an entire stranger. During a conversation of ten or fifteen minutes, while the lady sat on a sofa six or eight feet distant, suddenly her face became contorted, her body was seized with spasmodic jerks and twists, her eyes glared and closed, and then she sat quiet. In a few moments the writer was addressed from the body in broken English, and informed that the speaker was an Indian woman who had taken possession of madam's body while madam had gone to Kentucky to see her two sons who were in the army; that she — the Indian woman — would take care of the body until madam returned.

In five or eight minutes, however, the Indian woman said "I must go now." I replied, "Wait a minute." But she said, "I must go; madam is here, and must have her body." And instantly, with a few jerks and wriggles, she went out and madam evidently re-entered, inasmuch as she immediately resumed conversation where she had broken off prior to her departure.

Madam made no apology for her abrupt leave, nor did she intimate in any way that she had been absent. Neither did I allude to the incident. I did, however, inquire after her family, and learned that her two sons were in the army, as before stated.

Being already familiar with this phenomenon, I was not alarmed as many would have been.

Once I took a good Methodist friend to hear a lecture on Spiritualism. During the discourse a woman in the audience became entranced. When in her preliminary jerks and wriggles, my friend, who sat only a few feet distant, thought the woman had taken a fit, and in the kindness of his heart caught hold of her to save her from falling, and when the chairman requested him to be seated, he sat down in much confusion, greatly to the merriment of those who knew.

Logicians will not fail to discern a discrepancy in the foregoing remarks on the phenomenon of trance when considered in relation to a previous statement of what constitutes man, namely, life, matter and mind.

In explanation of trance phenomenon, it is stated that a person out of the flesh body can and ofttimes does take possession of the flesh body of another yet in the flesh.

This view of the case relegates the body to a mere possession of man, wholly ignoring the body as an integral part of man.

This possibly is the more philosophic view.

This point has been more fully explained elsewhere.

The material body, whether gross or ethereal, is so evanescent, so changeable when compared with life and mind, that we are warranted in the conclusion that the only real man consists of life and mind, that life never changes and mind ever accumulates, that man only uses matter to give expression to himself, as I use this paper.

CHAPTER XVII.

PHILOSOPHY OF HEALING.

THE healing of the sick and wounded of the present day is done by the same power and in the same mode in which healing was done in the days of Elijah, Elias, Jesus and his apostles.

We read that Jesus said he had no power of himself to heal; that all power to heal came from above; and that his disciples had, or could have, the same or like power from the same source, and might even excel him in such works.

This healing power from above comes from denizens of the aerial sphere, from those who have ceased to dwell in flesh and blood.

In the aerial spheres there exist many bands, so called, whose special work is healing. Each band is a regular combine for this one purpose. Again, there are those whose specialty is to traverse the earth and seek out and report those who dwell on earth who can be used as media for special purposes.

The healing virtue of any band or individual can only be effectively applied to those who can, to some extent, be magnetized — mesmerized, hypnotized — by those who endeavor to heal.

The healing is done by a dominant exertion of the will. The band — as a unit — wills it, and it is done.

It is an absolute fiat of will.

Success may be instantly complete; or it may be only an impulse in that direction which will continue until perfect success has crowned the effort.

This is the only source of power and mode of healing ever divulged or practised. Those who think Jesus is the only source or power forget that Jesus himself declared he had no healing power of himself, and added that all power to heal came from above.

We readily concede that hundreds, yea, thousands, have been healed while in the act of prayer to Jesus for the special favor; but it should be clearly understood, that when any one is in fervent prayer he is in a highly favorable condition to become charged with the magnetic aura generated and applied by the healing band, by virtue of which he is healed. And being thus healed, he gives all the glory to God or Jesus, never dreaming that he was healed by his brethren of the aerial sphere.

Nor does the glorious healing band take umbrage at being thus wholly ignored.

They remember that in days of yore they too dwelt in the flesh, and ignorantly believed that Jesus was the only source of all healing power.

Thence, in the exercise of charity, they have their reward in the good resulting therefrom, caring but little to whom the glory is given.

In the year 1861 the writer visited a distinguished healing medium, Dr. Newton, who had already healed thousands; and while waiting to go upstairs to the rooms in which the Doctor healed, a lady came leaping and screaming down stairs, crying out, "Glory to God! Glory to God! I am healed."

I tried to stop her in the hall, to question her; but she rushed past, and down the outer steps and up the street shouting, "Glory to God!" I afterwards learned that the lady had not walked one step, without crutches, for eight years. She left her crutches with the doctor. Well might she shout "Glory to God!" or anything that came into her mind. She was healed; that was everything.

A neighbor, well known to be a helpless cripple for many

years, who had slept in my house several nights, made an arrangement with a professed healing society — distant two hundred or more miles — to engage in prayer at eight o'clock P. M. every night, that he might be healed. After some weeks, he left home to visit a friend; and as eight o'clock P. M. arrived, he hobbled out on his two crutches to a wagon-shed to pray — it was raining at the time. While engaged in fervent prayer, lo! in a flash he was made whole. He immediately arose and returned to the house, leaping, and praising God.

In consequence, he became an indefatigable preacher of the gospel, according to Matthew, Mark, Luke and John.

Nothing has amazed the writer more than the ignorance displayed by educated people relative to miracles.

Materialists deny miracles altogether. Matthew Arnold says, "Miracles must go; pierced by Ithuriel's spear." Pierced by Matthew's tooth-pick rather.

The Protestant Church holds that the age of miracles has long since passed. The Catholic Church holds that miracles are not possible outside their holy sanctuary; notwithstanding, miracles are wrought every day in the year by people of all conditions.

It is a poor logic to ignore a phenomenon because we can't understand the *modus operandi* by which it is consummated. Facts are more conspicuous than law; and yet there is law in the working of all miracles. Not every numbskull, however, can entertain it.

All motion, all power, apart from purely physical phenomena, originate from *mind* in action as will.

Mind moves my hand as I write. The same power, acting under modified conditions, writes messages and paints pictures in colors, without visible means, within closed slates and hermetically sealed boxes.

The same power (will) disintegrates the molecules composing a solid iron ring and revolves the same back into a solid ring around a person's neck too small to be so placed by another process — all executed in a twinkle of time. All these are facts that have been as clearly demonstrated as any problem whatsoever.

Therefore, such power is amply sufficient to instantly change the abnormal condition of a function or tissue into normal relations of health, and thereby constitutes a miracle, in accordance with law of mind, with the fiat of will. "He spake, and it was done; He commanded, and it stood fast."

CHAPTER XVIII.

WORSHIP OF DEITY.

DEITY worship is founded on imagination, is but an exaggeration of hero worship.

Hero worship is not peculiar to man.

The lower animates indulge in like adulatory exercise.

Two lions will engage in furious combat in the presence of a lioness. One becomes champion, and instantly Mrs. Lioness fondles the hero and mates with him, wholly ignoring the vanquished.

Two ganders will engage in a desperate battle, one of which inevitably conquers. Instantly he is surrounded by every goose in the flock — the women of the tribe — each one gabbling vociferous congratulations to the champion, he standing erect, with arched neck, proud as a king; and king verily he is, while the conquered sneaks away alone, and not a goose will notice him for a month of Sundays.

Similar events often occur in Congress.

An honorable member gives battle — in words — to another; and, thinking he has discomfited his opponent, he stops. His friends instantly surround him and heap congratulations upon him, he standing erect, luminous with joy, while the ladies in the gallery extemporize kisses for him by handfuls.

Verily, man is but an animal; and although standing on the top round of the ladder of intelligence, he ofttimes manifests less sense and greater cruelty than those below him.

In all ages man has combined to make more effective his comprehensive knowledge to entrap, enslave and slay his fellows.

A crime not known among the lower animates.

Homo, are you proud of your distinctive characteristic?

CHAPTER XIX.

SENSE AND NONSENSE INTERMIXED.

WE read: "Except a man be born again, he cannot see the kingdom of God." "Except a man be born of water and of the Spirit, he cannot enter the kingdom of God."

Throughout the Scriptures, the kingdom of God, the kingdom of heaven, and the kingdom above, are convertible terms, meaning one and the same. The firmament is also called heaven; therefore, we may add, the kingdom of the firmament. Job speaks of the fowls of heaven, meaning the air.

Jesus' metaphorical manner of speaking led Nicodemus to think that Jesus referred to another birth, the same as the one he had already experienced.

Jesus, perceiving the error, explained to Nicodemus, in a roundabout way, how he could always know when any one was born of the spirit.

It is important just here to state that the term spirit, as here used, means *pneuma* (air), is often misused; therefore the term spirit is not always clearly understood; it is often misleading. Spirit in some cases means breath, but breath is always air; therefore, if we use the term air, all becomes plain and intelligible.

Jesus said to Nicodemus: "The wind bloweth where it listeth, thou canst not tell whence it cometh and whither it goeth; so is every one that is born of the spirit." That is, you cannot see the wind, nor can you see one that is born of the wind (air) or spirit.

The evident exegesis of this passage is, that a man must be

born twice; having already been born once — of water — he must also be born of the air, before he can enter the kingdom of air.

In the language of common parlance the air is above. Thence some commentators render the latter clause thus: Except a man be born from above, he cannot enter the kingdom above.

The errency of the Scriptures is conceded by all who have been as fortuitous as a pup nine days old. For example, Jesus is made to say: "That which is born of the flesh is flesh: that which is born of the spirit is spirit" (air).

This passage taken literally is bald nonsense.

It implies that man is flesh. Now everybody of common-sense knows that man is not flesh, nor ever could be, though he were born of the flesh a thousand times. Again: "That which is born of the spirit (air) is spirit," is air; surely man is not air though he were born of air a thousand times.

The evident meaning of the foregoing passage is, he that is born of the flesh abides in the flesh; he that is born of the air abides in the air.

Nothing more, nothing less.

The two immaterial components — life and mind — of man ever remaining invisible as wind, whether in the flesh or in the air.

With our present knowledge of life and the phenomenon miscalled death, it is clearly seen that the birth Jesus had reference to was the phenomenon named death.

The author who imputes these words to Jesus seems to have misunderstood Jesus as badly as Nicodemus.

The context by the author is tortured to show that Jesus had reference to the necessity of a conversion to the belief that Jesus alone had power to confer life eternal on man, otherwise all must die and be eternally damned.[1]

This view of this subject is too absurd to merit serious attention.

---

[1] Is it known that any one has ever been damned? And, if so, how was it made known?

Surely, it has been shown elsewhere that life *per se* is self-existent from everlasting to everlasting; that everlasting is an element of life that inheres in and to all animates whatsoever.

Indeed, the whole chapter is so replete with absurdities as to render the major part ridiculous; for example, "No man hath ascended up to heaven but the son of man (of God) who had come down from heaven, even the son of man which is in heaven."

Herein Jesus is represented as speaking of himself as the son of man (of God) who had come down from heaven, and who had gone up to heaven and who is in heaven; and yet, notwithstanding all this nonsense, Jesus is on earth talking with Nicodemus.

Sindbad never equalled this.

Whoever first told this story evidently had never heard of Enoch's ascension or Elijah's magnificent ascension to heaven in a chariot of fire.

Neither could he have heard of — or else had forgotten — Moses and Elias coming down from heaven to have a talk with this same Jesus relative to his approaching death at Jerusalem.

CHAPTER XX.

PLURALITY AND TRI-UNITY OF GOD.

SOMETHING never comes from nothing.

However, it is very difficult to find the germ of truth whence the above silly dogma originated.

In this case the immense exaggeration has well-nigh hidden the germ.

Possibly it arose from the misinterpreted, metaphysical disquisitions of Plato, who, about three hundred and sixty years before the advent of Jesus, had attributed to Deity several attributes which subsequent writers personified.

It would be a laborious task, and but little edifying, to trace the development of this foolish conception of two gods in one, or three in one, each equal in power and glory.

The reader who is not already familiar with them may be referred to Buckner, Guizot, Millman and Fuerback, especially the latter. All, however, are distinguished authors; and yet it may be truly said of them, as Job said to his pseudo comforters, "that they all multiply words without wisdom."

Sad to relate, however, that before this silly dogma became formulated as now found in the Nicene creed, the fierce contention of Christian factions sacrificed the life of thousands.

Every faction made a belief in some form of this dogma the standard of true faith.

It mattered but little whether one believed God to be two in one, or three in one; whether the Son was consubstantial with the Father or not; whether Homousius or Homoiusious was the correct rendering. The fires of persecution burned in all; and the dominant party invariably put to death all who differed with it.

This idea of a plural unity and tri-unity to many is ludicrously absurd. To many others it is divinely profound.

It has awed and deluded the Christian world for nearly two thousand years; and with many is yet paramount to all others.

All this lamentable persecution unto death of thousands arose from a misapprehension of what constituted both God and man.

Elsewhere we have seen that God the Father is life, including all the latent attributes of intelligence.

That man the Son is life also, including many of the active attributes of intelligence.

That God the Father embraces and includes all life. While man the Son embraces and includes only the spark, as it were, of life, by which he is energized.

That herein there is an essential difference; that the difference between action and inaction of intellectual attributes is not the difference of tweedle-dee and tweedle-dum, is not Homousius and Homoiusious over again; and that herein is discovered the germ of truth whence arose the whole conception of two gods in one person.

Elsewhere we trust we have shown how the Father is in the Son; also how the Son is in the Father. Our next effort will be to show how and whence the Holy Ghost originated and was denominated the third god in one.

Nowhere in the Jewish Scriptures do we read of God the Holy Ghost.

Nor is God the Holy Ghost ever prophesied of.

The psalmist asks God not to take his (God's) holy spirit from him.

The old sinner herein evidently believed that God possessed a holy spirit in the same sense as man possesses a liver; consequently, David could not have considered the Holy Ghost as the veritable God. The assertion that David spake by the mouth of the Holy Ghost is all bosh.

But in the New Testament Scriptures we read of the Holy Ghost many times repeated; always, however, in some way connected with Jesus.

True, we have a story put in shape, about forty years after the departure of Jesus from earth — told by somebody, no one knows who — that the child Jesus was begotten by the Holy Ghost overshadowing Mary his mother. B-A-H.

But Mary says the Holy Ghost didn't.

That settles it.

We learn through the imputed sayings of Jesus, how and wherein he and the Father were related.

By and from the same authority, we are told who the Holy Ghost is, and how Jesus and the Holy Ghost are related.

That we may gain a clear apprehension of the Holy Ghost, it becomes necessary to quote a few jumbled-up passages of Scripture relative thereto. If the quotations are not the words of Jesus, all the worse for those who misrepresent him and who persist in the misrepresentation.

Jesus is represented as conversing with his disciples on matters relating to life in the future, together with his approaching death.

Jesus, despairing of being able to make them have an intelligent understanding of the subject, and discerning that their hearts were filled with sorrow, said unto them: "I have yet many things to say unto you; but you cannot bear them now; nevertheless, I tell you the truth."

"It is expedient for *you* that *I* go away; for if I go not away, the comforter will not come unto you. But if I depart, I will send him unto you."

"He will guide you unto all truth; for he shall not speak of himself. But whatsoever he shall hear, that shall he speak; and he will show you things to come."

Why could the comforter, the Holy Ghost, not come until Jesus had departed?

Was it inexpedient for more than one god to leave heaven at one time, lest the Old Harry should re-enter and play havoc all around the throne, if Michael should happen to be away?

Why did not the Holy Ghost speak of himself?

Why did he only speak "whatsoever he heard?"

The Holy Ghost was the excarnated Jesus.

The excarnated Jesus could tell his disciples much more of life in the future, after his advent there and return, than he could before his departure, especially as he was going to tell them " whatsoever he heard."

The Ghost Jesus was a comforter, because in him they recognized their Lord who had been crucified, and whom they believed to be dead and buried. Verily, after Jesus had been born again, he could tell by experience what he saw and heard of life in the future.

" And when he had said this, he breathed on them, and said, Receive ye the Holy Ghost"; that is, receive ye me; the Holy Ghost and I are one.

Surely his breath was not the Holy Ghost.

The instant his body dissipated, he ceased to breathe; the instant he again re-inhabited his ethereal invisible body, breath ceases to be a necessity.

" If I go away, I will come again."

Verily, Jesus did come again.

Verily, he did come as a comforter.

" As they spake, Jesus *himself* stood in their midst, the doors being shut."

They were terrified — supposed they saw a spirit, a naughty, naughty spirit, a ghost.

But Jesus said: " Don't be afraid; behold my hands and my feet; that it is I myself."

" Handle me and see: a spirit hath not flesh and bones as ye see me have."

Herein Jesus discerned and catered to the ignorance of his disciples. His disciples, in common with others, believed that spirits, so-called, were different from men; were either angels or devils. Moreover, they thoroughly believed that Jesus was dead, and buried, and could by no possibility be alive; consequently, the person speaking must necessarily be a spirit, a ghost, without tangible body.

This view of this phenomenon was strictly in accordance with the intelligence of that day.

But we now know that even while on earth, we are all spirits — so called — clothed with flesh. We further know that the departed of earth may return and temporarily clothe themselves with flesh and bones and blood, that require breathing during the manifestation.

Ordinarily, those who have departed inhabit bodies that contain neither flesh nor bones.

When such return, they are wholly invisible to normal vision.

However, if Jesus had reappeared to his disciples in such a body, he would have been wholly invisible; consequently, would not have been recognized; and recognition was the all-important factor. Hence he materialized a body of flesh.

It was in materialized bodies that Moses and Elias manifested to Jesus, James and John; otherwise they could not have been seen by James and John; nor could they have heard Moses and Elias talk with Jesus.

We have seen, heard, handled, and been kissed and caressed by such celestial visitants. And, having related the fact, we feel a tinge of regret that we should have related to an infidel world a personal experience so sublime, so sacred, so sweet.

Those who are not familiar with materializations of our day — be they bishop, priest or layman — are wholly ignorant of the signification of the return of Moses, Elias and Jesus. This we assert with assurance, well remembering our own former ignorance.

Forty years we groped our way in the dark and cheerless valley of Orthodox bigotry and ignorance; consequently know what we assert.

It has been said, "that where ignorance is bliss, it is folly to be wise." We have never yet found ignorance a bliss. To us, knowledge alone giveth freedom; and freedom is bliss to all.

As to ghosts, all ghosts are holy, if good; all others are unholy.

CHAPTER XXI.

VAGARIES.

"Before the world was, I am."

As a matter of fact, the above declaration is not true.

It must not be forgotten that Jesus was an illiterate, hardworking young man, without opportunity to acquire knowledge of value.

All the beautiful and ofttimes profound sayings imputed to him resulted from impressions received by him from intelligences which existed outside of his organic being and wholly independent of his organism.

The difficulties experienced by exterior intelligences in giving correct impressions ofttimes result in vagaries that are fallacious or senseless.

Jesus, as an individual, had no existence prior to his organic being in flesh.

Jesus was and is a component of life, mind and matter; all of which existed from all eternity.

But life, mind and matter are not Jesus. His existence as a specific being began when life and mind first manifested animation and knowledge through matter.

Mind is not knowledge. Mind is an attribute of life by which knowledge is acquired, when life and mind are in organic union with matter.

So, too, in regard to this world; the matter of which it is composed existed from all eternity.

But this earth had no existence as a world prior to its planetary formation. Thus we see that the world, as such, had a beginning; that Jesus, as a being, had a beginning millions of years after the world was.

CHAPTER XXII.

MISAPPREHENSION.

"I have power to lay down my life; and I have power to take it up again."

The above declaration, imputed to Jesus, is a thoughtless, unwarranted assertion.

Jesus was and is a man, energized by life (by God, who is life). Surely, no one can take up or lay down God.

No man ever laid down life; nor did he ever take life up.

Neither the first nor the second birth is in any sense the result of a voluntary action. Birth in both cases results wholly from antecedent and present environment.

Life being a continuity from everlasting to everlasting, it follows that birth is but the result of life's specific organic union with matter, over which no sentient being has the least control.

All animate manifestations result from three factors, namely, life, mind and matter, two of which are always invisible.

When Jesus reappeared to his disciples, his presence was no evidence that he had taken up life again; but on the contrary, it was evidence that life in him had never been laid down, that he only had been transplanted from the visible body to an invisible body, and had again temporarily reinhabited a visible body for his disciples' special benefit.

How silly it is to say that Jesus was the first fruit of the dead, knowing that Moses and Elias had both manifested in flesh prior to the death of Jesus! While the assertion that Jesus was God, by whom the world was made and all that is therein, is too idiotic to be expressed outside an insane asylum.

The reappearance of Jesus to his disciples was exactly what is now known as materialization.

Materialization, however, is an improper term, without proper qualification.

The almanacs tell us the hour at which the sun sets and rises each day in the year; and yet all know that the sun neither rises nor sets.

This kind of information, however, subserves its purpose, yet is wholly misleading in fact; and if we knew it not, we should fail to enjoy, in contemplation, the magnificent motions of the planets of the solar system.

Spirits (persons) never materialize.

Spirits only manifest through material.

Spirit is life. Life is immaterial.

When excarnated man desires to manifest himself to man yet in the flesh, he is obliged to manifest through matter in his twofold capacity — life and intelligence.

When desirous of recognition, he manifests in his old body and garb, with which his friends in the flesh were once familiar. Saul knew Samuel by his mantle.

The disciples of Jesus knew him by his nail-prints.

We now know that it is a frequent occurrence for excarnated persons to be present in material bodies, and yet be wholly invisible to normal vision.

Being thus present is not a reincarnation, inasmuch as this kind of material body hath neither flesh nor blood nor bones.

This ethereal material body is the normal body inhabited by all denizens of the aerial sphere.

How glorious it must be and is, to inhabit a body wholly freed from all aches, pains and fevers that flesh, bones and blood are heir to!

A body so ethereal as to be almost (or altogether) freed from the attraction of gravity, and yet which possesses material sufficient to give more exquisite sensibility to all desires, and through which all thoughts are more readily and more sensibly transmitted to others in the same condition and sphere than

MISAPPREHENSION.

words and desires are transmitted to friends in our present sphere.

While in the flesh we walk, run and climb by will power, exerted and operating through muscle at great expenditure of both. When freed from the flesh, by will power alone we can speed across continents and seas with the velocity of thought.

Twenty-six years ago the writer sat for a photographic likeness of himself, at midday.

Two images appeared on the negative.

The likeness of a man — dim, but distinct in outline — stood erect in front, in a position that hid from view my entire right side.

This dim likeness of a man on the negative could not possibly have been a re-development of an old picture on an old plate, inasmuch as the ghost picture was on top, whereas a re-development of an old picture on an old plate must, of necessity, be beneath or behind the sitter.

The writer again sat, and again two pictures appeared on the negative.

The ghost picture in this case was the image of a lady with long curls, who stood behind with her left hand extended and resting gracefully upon and in front of the writer's shoulder, thus showing that in this case the invisible person was behind; her left hand was in front, thus again demonstrating that the double picture could in no possible manner be a re-development of an old picture.

It is needless to state that no person was visibly present to either the operator or subject; and yet it was a clear double demonstration that invisible friends were present in material bodies.

The writer has never met a photographer so near the bristle plane as to assert that original pictures of persons could be taken without their presence in material bodies.

Art photography has become so perfected that the sensitized plate brings to view multitudes of stars that have hitherto eluded vision, aided by the most powerful telescopes.

This beautiful photographic phenomenon further demonstrates that we of the flesh are ever plainly visible to our departed invisible friends.

This invisible lady, standing behind the chair, laid her left hand upon the writer's right shoulder as gracefully and naturally as any lady could have done while in the flesh.

Could anything offer a greater inducement to correct deportment on our part, than to realize that our loved departed may ever be present with us, and can read all our thoughts and see all our actions?

Ah! we ofttimes grieve away our dearly beloved.

CHAPTER XXIII.

WHAT IS SIN?

"Sin is any want of conformity to, or transgression of the law of God."

Yes, that is it, exactly.

But what is the law of God?

To ascertain the law of God, a prerequisite is to learn who and what God is.

Heretofore we have shown that God is life — nothing more, nothing less.

Could not be more, could not be less.

Without life naught, except matter.

With life, united with matter, everything that *is* originated, excepting only life and matter.

Thence, in life and matter all vegetates, all animates live, move and have existence.

Could anything exceed life in abstract greatness and grandeur?

We have also shown that life and matter in union begat desire to maintain the specific form of union; that specific forms of union were the results of specific environment, together with parental impress.

This desire to maintain the specific form is manifested in all forms of union.

Why this desire, we discern not; but notwithstanding, all animate life proves this fact.

We have further seen, that to maintain the specific organic form of union, a constant aggregation of matter is an irrevocable requisite; that as soon as aggregation ceases, the specific form disintegrates to extinction.

Now, then, any omission or commission of an act that puts in jeopardy the specific form of union of life with matter is sin against life, is sin against God.

Every act of commission that tends to perpetuate the specific union is an act in conformity with the law of life, with the law of God.

Thence we again inquire, What is sin? Sin is any omission or commission of an act that tends toward, or destroys, any specific form of union of life with matter.

When anything is done or omitted whereby our own life in the flesh, or the life of another is endangered or impaired or evicted, we sin against life, against God.

Again, when anything is done or omitted that endangers, reduces or destroys happiness in the flesh, of ourselves or others, we sin against life, against God.

Matthew Arnold — rich in literature, but poor in logic — aspiring to elucidate and embody a supernatural something other than God, disdaining to use the hackneyed phrases of others, invents a phraseology of his own, by which he vainly hopes to escape the ridicule he heaps upon others in the same dilemma, and prates of "an enduring power, not of ourselves, that makes for righteousness."

In view of facts, both logical and demonstrable, it would be hard to find a phraseology sillier or more ambiguous.

The old familiar passage "that God works within, to will and to do, at his own good pleasure," is far preferable, and is beautiful when properly understood.

If the writer may be permitted to paraphrase the latter, he would read it thus: Life and mind, in action, work within with pleasure, to do whatsoever environment requires to prolong life in the flesh.

This rendering of the sentiment is logical, is based upon facts established by the observation of thousands.

That will is a power and is only mind in action, is patent to all.

That change of environment necessitates a change of doing,

WHAT IS SIN?

is also patent to all; that doing, under the change of circumstances, is a pleasure, is patent to all.

As a rule, however, environment is something over which individuals have no control; consequently, a sudden change of environment may be so excessive as to render individuals unable to fulfil the new demands of life. Hence, eviction from the flesh domicile is inevitable; and under such conditions eviction is not chargeable to individuals; consequently, is not sin against life, against God.

Geological and paleontological science teach that the earth has repeatedly been subject to cataclysmal changes so great and sudden that will power exerted with all its might failed to meet the demands. These changes have resulted in the extinction of numerous species of animates.

This sudden change of environment is the only cause of extinct fauna and flora found in any part of the earth.

But to return to the further elucidation of "What is sin?" We again inquire of Jesus.

He is infallible authority with millions; therefore it is the part of wisdom to quote largely from his reputed sayings, in verification of our conclusions.

We read in the Gospel according to Matthew, that "they brought unto Jesus a man sick of the palsy."

Jesus said unto him, "Son, be of good cheer; thy *sins* be forgiven thee."

The scribes said, "This man blasphemes."

Jesus replied, "Think you it is easier to say, "Thy sins be forgiven thee, or to say, Arise and walk? But that you may know that the Son of Man hath power on earth to forgive sin." Not the Son of God, you observe.

Then said Jesus to the sick of the palsy, "Arise! take up thy bed and go. And he arose and departed."

This man, be it observed, was not charged with sin against the Hebrews' God, or any other god. He was not charged with being a sinner in any manner.

However, being sick of the palsy was evidence that he, or

his parents or ancestors, had sinned against life, had sinned against the laws of health, and thereby and to that extent was unable to enjoy life in the *flesh;* and that was the *sin,* and the only sin, Jesus had reference to.

"The multitude saw it and glorified God, who had given such power to man." Not to Jesus alone, but to man.

Herein we find that healing disease and the forgiveness of sin were one and the same as apprehended by Jesus.

Nowhere do we find Jesus forgiving any kind of sin, except that against life in the flesh, whereby life in the flesh becomes impaired and detrimental to the enjoyment of life in the flesh.

The blind man, the dumb man, the young woman sick of the fever were all diseases of the flesh, and all were sins against life in the flesh, against God in the flesh.

"He (Jesus) healed all manner of disease."

Not all manner of sins.

Some kinds of sin are irreparable; consequently cannot be forgiven; for example, sins against offspring, murder, theft, robbery, slander, adultery and all such; therefore, take heed.

We read that Jesus said, "All manner of sins may be forgiven, except sin against the Holy Ghost."

Now what is sin against the Holy Ghost? or was he erroneously reported?

Herein Jesus evidently did not understand what he was saying; possibly he was slightly impressed to give expression of his future return in ghostly form. For, as a matter of fact, there is no Holy Ghost *per se.*

The Ghost Jesus may be more holy than others, but all good people's ghosts are holy, more or less, according as they have been good or bad while in the flesh.

If the above saying imputed to Jesus has any sense in it, he evidently had reference to his return, after his departure from the flesh.

We now know that it is wholly impossible for any one in the flesh to injure, to sin against any one out of the flesh.

WHAT IS SIN?

In other words, it is wholly impossible to sin against any kind of ghost, either holy or unholy.

However, it is very true, that we may and ofttimes do grieve away our good ghosts — our good friends in the aerial sphere — when they desire to impress us with edifying thoughts and good deeds; and thus grieve them away to our own detriment, but not by any manner of means to their injury.

When there is no injury done, there is no sin committed.

If we persist in grieving away our good friends of the aerial sphere, who wish to impress us with knowledge, for example, that would prevent our own premature departure from the flesh ere we had fulfilled our possible mission here, we thus sin against ourselves and the whole race of man, inasmuch as the work we should have done while in the flesh remains undone forever; and humanity has thus, and to that extent, been defrauded forever, inasmuch as there is no power existing whereby we may be again restored to the flesh under the same environment.

When the thief on the cross, in great agony of pain, appealed to Jesus, in like condition, for relief, Jesus did not say, "Thy sins be forgiven thee."

The only help or comfort Jesus could give under the circumstances was to assure the thief that, "To-day thou shalt be with me in paradise."

The thief was not suffering from disease of the flesh. Jesus could not abrogate his sin of theft; that act was past remedy.

The thief may have got it into his head — the same as Orthodoxy — that Jesus had power to forgive all manner of sins, instead of all manner of disease; but he was wofully disappointed, and so will Orthodoxy be. The thief on the other side had the more level head.

And yet, doubtless, the thief experienced a measure of comfort, to be assured that he and Jesus were going to the same place on the same day. It certainly would have so affected the writer.

Observe that Jesus said "to-day" — not to-morrow, not on

the third day, but "*to-day* thou shalt be with me." Where? Not in the grave, not in hell. Nor did Jesus say, To-day thy soul shall be with my soul in paradise. Nor did he say, To-day thy spirit shall be with my spirit in paradise. But, To-day you and I shall both together be in paradise.

Paradise is supposed to be a place of happiness. I think it is.

Now, when Jesus and the thief appeared in paradise (in the aerial sphere), each was the selfsame individual as when on the cross, except only they were freed from the flesh and from the pains experienced in the flesh. Jesus was still the meek and lowly honest man; while the thief was still the thief, and would remain so forever.

He could not repair the injury he had done another; therefore he remained a thief debtor forever. Nothing existed here or there wherewith he could obliterate the thief mark.

A sapling with bark bruised may grow to be a large tree, several hundred years old.

New wood and new bark may have covered over and entirely obliterated the appearance of a bruise on the surface; but in the heart the old bruise remains all the same, visible to clairvoyant vision.

Theft is sin against another; and although we may do many acts of kindness for reparation while in the flesh — may, like the new wood and bark, succeed in covering over, but not in healing, the wound — yet, when transplanted to the aerial sphere, the hideous thing is seen by all.

CHAPTER XXIV.

SUNS, PLANETS AND SATELLITES OF THE UNIVERSE.

MATTER, viewed in the aggregate throughout the universe, is a unit, is governed by the dominant forces inherent therein.

All suns throughout the universe originated, developed and exist under the same general forces; while each exists under special forces peculiar to its own special environment.

Planets throughout the universe originate, develop and exist under the same general forces; while each exists under special forces peculiar to the environment of each.

Satellites also originate, develop and exist under the same general and inherent forces by which planets are governed and exist, with some additional forces added thereto, consequent on having passed the planetary stage.

Therefore, there is a sameness of all suns, a sameness of all planets and a sameness of all satellites; each, however, possessing peculiar characteristics arising from its peculiar environment.

Life, in the abstract, is a unit, is self-existent; consequently it is the same throughout the universe, and must necessarily manifest under the same or similar conditions through matter. Nevertheless, each vegetate and animate manifests life under special conditions arising from the special environment, by which each is given a special organism.

The conditions requisite to manifestations of life throughout the universe are much the same.

Life animate requires blood heat, at about 98° Fahrenheit, and this degree of heat is maintained alike in the torrid and frigid zones.

The degree of heat upon each planet is determined by the magnitude and distance of the planet from its sun, and the density of the atmosphere at the surface of the planet.

The greater the mass of the planet, the denser the air — consequent upon the greater force of gravity. Notwithstanding the great distance Jupiter is from the sun, his great mass gives greater attraction and denser atmosphere; which may give as great, or greater, heat on his surface than is found on the earth's surface.

The telescope and spectroscope tell us very little of the physical constitution and condition of suns, planets and satellites — and absolutely nothing in regard to life vegetate and animate.

All in regard to life on other planets, thus far, has been guess-work. But as like causes always produce like results, we may reasonably infer that life exists on all planets whose surface conditions are similar to the earth's.

The adaptation of life manifestations to heat and cold has a range of about 300° Fahrenheit. We read that Indian children in Alaska play barefooted on snow, with the thermometer 30° below zero. This seems hardly possible; still it emphasizes the extreme range of adaptation of life manifestations to environment.

The writer has breathed air 28° below zero, the sensation being much the same as swallowing an icicle.

Now, if denizens of the aerial sphere of earth are almost or altogether independent of, and freed from, the power of gravity; if they have the facility of locomotion, as elsewhere stated; if they possess an ethereal body in which dwells all sensibility, all knowledge in all its fulness as when in the flesh; and if we do receive thousands of communications from friends who inhabit the aerial sphere, — then why, oh, why, do they not tell us of the conditions and peculiarities of phenomena on other planets and satellites?

Well, there are many logical reasons why not.

We have shown that no manifestation of life can occur except by and through matter; that no manifestation of intelligence can occur except life is present. We further know that oxygen is requisite to the maintenance of life manifestations, and possibly to the very existence of life. We also know that interplanetary and stellar space is almost a void, consequent upon the rarity of matter therein. We, moreover, know that inhabitants of the aerial sphere are subjected in some degree to all the laws and forces to which they were subject while in the flesh. Hence, they may be unable to pass beyond the earth's aerial sphere; and if able to pass, owing to the rarity of the matter and consequent lack of oxygen, may under such conditions become wholly unable to manifest life, without which no manifestation of intelligence can occur; and yet life in those regions may exist in much the same condition as life in a frozen fish.

Again, we have shown that all inanimate objective phenomena in this sphere become subjective phenomena in the aerial sphere; that we can only perceive subjective phenomena that are representative of the objective phenomena with which we have previously become familiar.

Thence it follows, that although denizens of earth's aerial sphere may succeed in visiting other planets, they may yet perceive but little, consequent upon the phenomena there being so very different from phenomena with which they have been familiar here. For example, an inhabitant of the tropics, who never saw ice here in objective form could not perceive ice in subjective form there.

Denizens of earth's aerial sphere would necessarily become denizens of Jupiter's aerial sphere; therefore could only discern the objective phenomena on Jupiter, as a reflex in the aerial sphere in subjective form.

Denizens of earth's aerial sphere can discern objective phenomena on earth, but can only give expression of such by coming *en rapport* with persons yet in the flesh, and can only come *en rapport* with those who have a magnetic affinity; hence, when our people visit Jupiter, they find no one there whose affinity permits them to come *en rapport*, and thus fail to clearly discern (so as to give expression of) objective phenomena on Jupiter.

Hence the many reasons why we cannot have reliable information of other planets from inhabitants of earth's aerial sphere.

Many years ago, in answer to a question asked by the writer, he was told by one who appeared to be an intelligent resident of the air, that the sun's atmosphere prevented him from visiting the sun, for observation; consequently, he could tell nothing about the sun. Notwithstanding, we have a vast amount of Spiritualistic literature — so called — that tells us much about the inter-exchange of visitants from the sun and other planets with earth.

A gentleman friend, yet in the flesh, tells me that he is a reincarnation; that formerly he was a resident of Jupiter; that his sweetheart followed him to this planet, and is at present a resident of earth's aerial sphere, and pays him daily visits. He honored me with the presentation of a photographic copy of her likeness, recently taken in oil by spirit artists.

Reader, this is not all nonsense.

A germ of truth lurks therein. If you have a metaphysical trend of mind, seek for it; when found, you will be delighted.

"Then came Jesus, the doors being shut, and stood in their midst."

That is it exactly.

But how did he get in?

The doors being shut, how did he enter?

Well, in a strict sense, Jesus was and is a component of life, mind and intelligence, all of which are immaterial.

Mind includes thought; thought goes wheresoever we will it.

Jesus entered in like manner, as immaterial thought. He clothed himself with flesh and raiment after he entered, as a prerequisite to being recognized and to the utterance of speech.

Bear in mind that life and speech can only be expressed through matter.

This strange phenomenon has become quite familiar to thousands in our day.

No one can believe it without seeing it.

Many who do see it still disbelieve it.

The most profound adept and expert fails to comprehend it.

The phenomenon, however, remains a fact, transcendent in grandeur; and it may be verified by all.

CHAPTER XXV.

BEGINNING WITHOUT ENDING.

"NAKED came I out of my mother's womb, and naked shall I return thither."

No book in the Old Testament Scriptures contains more beautiful and profound sayings than the book imputed to Job.

The above quotation, however, is neither beautiful nor true, and yet it has been reiterated from thousands of pulpits for more than three thousand years, as an embodiment of profound wisdom that all should heed.

The accumulation of knowledge overturns many cherished sayings.

Neither Job, nor any other person, ever returned to his mother's womb.

If Job spake in a figurative sense of Mother Earth, the declaration was equally false, in fact and philosophy; and being false, it was pernicious in effect.

There is no axiom of metaphysical science more clearly established by experience, and confirmed by the rigid philosophy of phenomena, than that man's advent in organic form, in matter, is the initial of constant and continuous acquisition.

Every hour after his advent adds to his possessions in some shape and kind. Every thought suggested by nature or art, — everything seen, felt or heard — adds thereto; all of which he possesses and holds throughout eternity.

"What!" inquires bigotry, "can a man, when he departs the flesh, take with him into the invisible sphere of life all his houses and lands, all his gold and silver, and stocks and stuffs of all kinds?" Yes; all have become representative of his personality. A man is known by his possessions. All of his objective possessions become, like unto his mental possessions, subjective in form ; and, as such, they go with him wheresoever he goeth.

When a landed proprietor visits his banker in the city, he carries with him, in subjective form, all his objective possessions; and when the banker visits in the country, he carries with him all his gold and stocks, in subjective form. The land-lord and gold-lord are esteemed in accordance with the estimated value of their possessions, and the use they make of them.

So, too, when man crosses over the figurative River Jordan, all his objective possessions are invoiced to his credit and debit, according to their subjective value, together with all his mental acquirements; and in that shape, they go over with him and cling to him forever.

The good and bad alike.

Not all the blood of bulls and goats, nor the wicked shedding of an innocent brother's blood, can wash away or blot out one "jot or tittle" of all.

Thence, as all our thoughts and deeds done in the flesh ever remain with us, what pain, what so row, what mortification must ensue to many, when all are clearly seen by friends and foes!

A few may point with pride to records of deeds done; but many will hang their heads in shame.

But inasmuch as all have sinned, inasmuch as fortuitous environments have hedged some while unfortuitous environments have hedged others, charity — sweet charity, pearl of all virtues — eventually enfolds all, like a mother's love.

CHAPTER XXVI.

DESIGN OR ACCIDENT, WHICH?

ALL natural phenomena are logically divided into two classes, namely, matter phenomena and life phenomena.

Matter phenomena manifest neither life, nor intelligence, nor sensation.

Life phenomena manifest growth, motion, sensation and volition.

Man in his primitive ignorance conceived the idea that all phenomena beyond his power of production were produced by superior beings, possessed by superior intelligence and power. All such phenomena were imputed to gods; hence arose the multitudinous gods of barbaric nations.

However, as man evolved intelligence through experience with matter, he discarded his many gods, and substituted for all, one only God, supreme in intelligence and power over all.

Supreme wisdom and power imply law, order, harmony and goodness.

Parrots in literature, science and theology gabble and babble much of law and order — much of wisdom, of the evidence of design shown in all of nature's operations.

To logical minds, however, there is not one item of law, order, harmony or wisdom evidenced in all the works of Nature.

Instead of harmony, a state of warfare exists throughout the universe; all matter phenomena result from the blind, senseless energies inherent in matter; these forces dominate and rule all. When we consider the senseless, antagonistic forces resident in matter, it is readily seen that continuous warfare is inevitable.

The primary and dominant factors of matter are gravity and heat, expressed by attraction and repulsion; the legitimate result of these two antagonistic forces is motion in opposite directions. This antagonism is constant. Harmony can never result from constant warfare. Antagonism must cease ere harmony can manifest her genial mien.

No atom in the universe is freed from these two forces; and inasmuch as every atom possesses polarity (positive and negative), it follows that, under the potency of these two forces, every atom is constantly changing its polarity, and consequent relation with all other atoms, resulting in constant motion of all matter in the universe, and thus necessitating constant change of all phenomena. Hence the infinite variety and degrees of phenomena, and the impossibility of an exact repetition of any phenomena; thus precluding law, order or harmony always and everywhere.

On the contrary, however, all art shows unmistakable evidence of wisdom, of design, of harmony in all minute details.

The watch, for example, is designed to show forth passing time in hours, minutes and seconds, elapsing fifty to one hundred years; and yet the watch manifests no intelligence *per se*, only the intelligence of the designer. But if, after completion, the designer should suddenly and with intent smash the watch into fragments, would he not justly be considered an idiot? Furthermore, suppose he had designed and made a thousand million watches — all beautiful and different of design, all fulfilling their designed work to perfection — and, lo, without apparent cause, he should smash them all to flinders, would he not justly be considered a dangerously mad lunatic?

Now, if a supreme designer of natural phenomena be conceded, he does just what the watchmaker is supposed to have done, but in a thousand million times more aggravated degree; a thousand million times is he a greater criminal.

Those thousand million watches had no sensation, knew naught of their destruction; whereas the supreme designer of natural phenomena designs thousands of millions of sentient beings, and designs each a body in which to abide, endows each with a supreme desire to so abide. Each is designed and endowed with exquisite loves, with poignant sensations of pleasure. The earth is clothed with verdure; the hills and vales are decked with fruits and flowers — when, lo, this all-wise, all-powerful designer sends a frost, a flood, a famine, a cyclone, an earthquake, and remorselessly destroys all!

The history of the earth shows that such calamities have been of frequent occurrence.

Oh, who can adequately realize the anguish of a thousand million sentient beings violently bereft of body!

In 1876 two hundred and fifty thousand human beings in Calcutta perished by a cyclone.

In 1878 thirteen million human beings perished by famine in China. Doubtless, a thousand million other animates perished with them.

September 1, 1895. Stamford, North America. Samuel Searle, age forty, and son, age five, were out sailing; the boat capsized. Mr. Searle started to swim to shore with the son on his back, when a flash of lightning struck them, and both were instantly killed.

Was it so designed?

September 5, 1895. Baltimore, Md., North America. The funeral of Mary Browne had entered the Mount Winans Cemetery; the hearse had just stopped at the open grave, when a flash of lightning struck the driver, Wm. Alsup, and he fell back dead.

Was it so designed?

May 23, 1890. Berlin, Germany. In the village of St. Mahlen the people were in church, praying for the cessation of a hail-storm that was doing great damage. While in the act of prayer, lightning struck the church, instantly killing four and seriously wounding twenty. In the wild rush for the door two children were trampled to death.

Was it so designed?

A year or more since, a beautiful young lady, while bathing

off the coast of Maine, North America, a monster *devil-fish* reached up his long arm and pulled her underneath the waves.

Was it so designed?

Thousands of such cases occur every year.

Next let us consider the insect realm.

The cicada is a beautiful, blithesome little songster during bright summer days; less harmful than a sucking dove; lives entirely on vegetables. The sandhill wasp — also beautiful, with a long, slender body and crow-black, glossy sheen — is the cruel enemy of the cicada; and when in its carol glee the wasp pounces upon it and stabs it — but not to kill — and drags it to the wasp's den to feed the young larva, and thus the little innocent cicada is slowly eaten, while yet alive, for weeks ere it dies.

Was it so designed?

A large species of brown spider lays its eggs and incloses them in a silken ball, and with its many legs and arms hugs the ball to its abdomen to keep it warm; and when the eggs are hatched, five hundred or a thousand of the brood attach themselves to, and feed upon, the mother for weeks, until she is entirely consumed.

Was it so designed?

Three-fourths of all animates live by eating others.

Was it so designed?

Hence our only escape, only relief from the hideous sickening facts is to relegate all natural phenomena to accident — to blind, senseless energies resident in matter.

When we consider the class designated as *life phenomena*, we perceive the same lack of design anterior to the evolution of mind consequent upon the union of life with matter.

In vegetation we see life phenomena in their lowest, crudest forms; and although evolution is perceived in some degree, it is clearly traceable to the changed conditions of matter. But when intelligence intervenes, as shown by art, by intelligence, by culture, we find flowers and fruits beautified and improved.

So, too, with the class fauna.

In marine habitats, we find but little, if any, evolution, owing to the almost unchangeable conditions in which they live; whereas land habitats have undergone marvellous changes in structure and habits, owing to the many changes through which the matter of the earth's crust has passed.

Now, although change of matter is the dominant factor necessitating change of animate structure for adaptation to new conditions, yet mind — intelligence evolved from life, consequent of changed conditions — is also a factor that modifies structure and habits.

The primitive split-foot horse, if such ever was, shows marvellous evolution, necessitated by changed conditions of matter; however, had he lacked intelligence of adaptation, he could not have survived.

A brood sow, confined to a lot in which a large steam-boiler was in operation, having dropped her pigs one cold day in midwinter, manifested much wisdom by carrying straw and placing it under the boiler until warmed, and then carrying it to her brood's nest to warm her progeny.

The marvellous improvement in animates consequent upon intelligent adaptation to the necessities of the situation is a manifestation of design — of art — as clearly as their further improvement owing to the applied intelligent culture by man.

Yea, the energies resident in matter dominate all animates in all their manifestations.

Hippocrates says, "You will find, as a rule, that the form of the body and the disposition of the mind correspond to the nature of the country."

CHAPTER XXVII.

CHANCE VERSUS LAW.

"TIME and chance happeneth to all."

The universe of matter, considered in the aggregate, remains substantially the same in quantity throughout eternity.

Not one atom added or subtracted. Nothing gained, nothing lost.

Progression and retrogression are apparently equal; some stars and planets progressing, others retrogressing; the planet Earth evolving, the planet Moon resolving.

On the contrary, however, mind evolved from life in its domain of action is ever progressing, is ever accumulating, is ever increasing in knowledge and consequent power through experience with matter.

The magnetic impress of mind upon matter prevents matter from ever again relapsing into exact previous conditions; and although matter may be resolved into its primary elements, to all chemical and physical appearance it yet retains the magnetic impress of mind in some degree.

The inerrancy of the Bible is believed by millions; and yet no book contains more foolish and contradictory statements. The above quotation, however, embodies much profound wisdom. It is one of the few philosophic truths found within its cover.

The inherent energies of matter, elsewhere explained, by and through which matter is convulsed and tossed, whence all phenomena are evolved and expressed, are so infinite in kind, so varied in degree, so unstable in location of operations, as to render it wholly impossible to reduce and forecast therefrom definite results by observation or mathematical analysis.

If it were possible to reduce the operations of these inherent, blind forces of matter to mathematical formulas, it could be foretold when and where every drop of rain and flake of snow would fall; also how many drops and flakes would fall in the same spot.

With the foregoing premises in view, it is clearly seen that chance is the only word expressive of natural phenomena, as regards time, location and degrees of results.

Gravity is the only one of all the inherent forces of matter that is constant and true to its own energy; and yet, owing to the constant changing of matter from solid to liquid and vapor, and the reverse, the results therefrom are as varied as the winds and waves.

Gravity ever strives for an equilibrium, and is ever thwarted by heat energy, as a repellant of centripetal force.

Heat is as constant and potent a factor in the production of phenomena as gravity, and infinitely more varied. The legitimate results of each force is motion in opposite directions. This constant warfare creates confusion as to results; whereby, in time, chance happeneth to all.

Each force by which matter is affected would produce definite results if it were not thwarted by others; but as each force is constant and antagonistic, definite results are not possible. The principal field of battle, as relates to the earth, is in the air. Heat and gravity are the principal, and possibly the sole, factors of all phenomena, except life and life phenomena. Owing to the exceeding sensibility of air to change of temperature and its capacity of high velocity of motion, it is wholly impossible to forecast results therefrom. Floods, famines, cyclones, earthquakes and volcanic eruptions are all the results of the varied contests of heat and gravity; consequently, these two forces account for all phenomena, except those wherein life is manifested.

Those who believe in a Supreme Being, infinite in wisdom,

power and love, find it a logical necessity to assume foreordination; after which, as a corollary, it becomes necessary to add thereto special providences, to meet what seem special emergencies. For example, June 22, 1892, two little boys climbed a tree to rob a bird's-nest; lightning struck the tree and killed both little boys. According to popular theology, this was a special providence. June 7, 1892, the writer found an oriole's nest, blown from a tree in the door-yard, in which three little birds had perished; this was foreordination, according to Orthodoxy. We are told that every sparrow that falls is known and seen by the all-wise, all-powerful, all-loving Creator. But wherein had the little birds sinned, to whom life in the flesh was so sweet? Again, were the eggs more sacred than the brood? If not, why kill the two little boys whom, we are told, Jesus died to save? Surely a being of infinite love, wisdom and power would not have killed the boys and birds to make the hearts of parents bleed.

To logical minds, it is clearly seen that all phenomena, except the first two, life and matter, result from chance victories of these two forces.

Owing to the diversity of the earth's surface — including hill, dale, lake and ocean — together with the earth's axial and orbital motions, solar heat is constantly creating high-pressure and low-pressure areas in the vaporous ocean by which the earth is surrounded, in thousands of different localities, thousands of miles apart; all of which are constantly changing their relative positions in as many different directions, with a speed varying from one mile to three hundred miles an hour.

Now, when we for a moment consider the varied directions and velocities at which these high and low pressure areas are constantly being shifted in their relative positions, and the consequent changes in the directions and velocities of air motions, we see how lame, how futile all weather prophecy must be; and yet we have weather prophets dotted all over this continent, including the august Sanhedrim enthroned at the seat of national government.

The aerial ocean, unlike the aqueous ocean, is exceedingly elastic, is very sensitive to changes of temperature; the least change of temperature in any part destroys the equilibrium of the whole vaporous ocean. Its great elasticity enables it to instantly rush furiously, in order to restore the equilibrium; and in its haste and zeal to fill up a low, it overdoes the work, and creates a high, that is equally destructive to equilibrium. Thus, ever striving to restore an equilibrium that never existed within the realm of planet or star.

Now, inasmuch as there are thousands — yea, millions — of these disturbing areas scattered over earth and ocean surfaces, if we consider the results in detail, it is clearly seen that it could not be otherwise than that "chance happeneth to all." For example:

June 9, 1892, Oil City, North America, totally destroyed by flood and fire; sixty lives lost.

June 13, 1892, Chicago, North America, struck by a tornado; eight killed and many wounded.

Same day, at Melias, Spain, a church was struck by lightning; ten killed, twenty-eight wounded, while saying mass.

June 14, 1892, Galva, North America, struck by a cyclone; twenty-eight killed, hundreds wounded, entire village destroyed.

Same day, at Galesburg, North America, a terrific storm; three churches torn to pieces during service; several killed and many wounded.

June 15, 1892, St. Rose, Canada, North America, struck by a cyclone; houses, animals and people carried great distances and dashed to death.

June 16, 1892, at Baladona, Spain, a terrible hurricane; eight killed, hundreds wounded, two factories torn to pieces.

Same day, at St. Paul, North America, a cyclone; one hundred killed, hundreds wounded.

Same day, at Union Town, North America, Mrs. Yowler killed by lightning; three children by her side were not hurt.

June 25, 1892, Matanza Island desolated by a deluge; one hundred and fifty people drowned.

Same day, at Cuba Village, North America, a terrible tornado; every house in the village destroyed.

November, 1891, in Japan, forty thousand people perished by an earthquake.

Similar accidents by chance could be enumerated by thousands every year, many of which occur simultaneously, thousands of miles apart.

Elsewhere we have shown that heat and gravity, expressed through matter, give us every variety and degree of environment; that special environment differentiates all vegetable and animal phenomena; that metaphysical phenomena are evolved from the physical; that the status of mind and morals is determined by quality of environment; that mind has not evolved sufficiently to control matter in the aggregate; that life *per se*, with mind embodied in a latent state, awaits the proper conditions of matter, by chance produced, whereby it (life) may seize the favorable condition and moment to express its presence and power to control a moiety of matter in a limited degree and in a limited time.

As a cork upon the waves and a thistle-down in the wind, even so are all phenomena the sport of chance.

Profoundly realizing the almost infinite contingencies that inevitably arise on every hand, it is clearly seen that matter is not governed by mind, except in an infinitely small degree; that harmony is unperceived throughout the universe. However, as in music, numberless discordants produce perceptible concords, — at best, a jargon that makes a highly cultured melodist shiver, — even so is the harmony of phenomena.

Indeed, the whole philosophy of phenomena is constituted of numberless ifs. For example:

If the members of the solar system maintained forever the same relation to the sun and each other, if the infinite number of solar systems did the same, if all systems maintained the same relation to each other forever, if the primary elements of each system and of each member of each system remained the same forever, then evidence of the law of harmony might be proclaimed.

But inasmuch as every system and every member of every system is constantly changing its relations to all others, as every atom of each system and member is constantly changing relations with all other atoms, it inevitably follows that every manifestation of physical and metaphysical phenomena must be different from all preceding phenomena, that every manifestation of life necessarily differs from all preceding manifestations, that exact environment can never again be repeated, though trillions of æons roll away; therefore, definite results can never be forecast nor ought to be expected.

Nature includes all of life and all of matter.

Life ever struggles, not to exist, but to manifest its existence and to maintain the manifestation. When conditions are favorable, life manifests in forms of beauty and utility.

When conditions are unfavorable, life manifests in forms that are hideous and pernicious. For example:

In valleys where soil is rich and air salubrious, trees of magnificent height and proportions grow; whereas, on bleak mountains, trees grow stunted and scraggy. Again, in temperate zones, conditions being favorable, men and women grow shapely and lovely; while in frigid and torrid zones men and women grow hideous in form and feature; life *per se* being the same in all these varied conditions.

Emerson said that "divinity was in the atoms." He would have been more edifying had he said that life was in the atoms. Divinity is a figment, whereas life is manifested all around.

Thus, by the logic of chance we gain a clue why so many hideous and pernicious things exist that possess land and water, and are naught but unmitigated pests to higher and more beauteous forms of life.

It is silly to assume that a being infinite in wisdom, power and love did, with pleasure or malice intent, bring forth the octopus, cobra, tarantula and hosts of similar animates, together with the whole parasitic world, all of which inflict untold misery upon higher orders of creatures.

We submit that, inasmuch as infinite varieties and degrees of environment exist by chance, there is no room for surprise at infinite results, including the hideous and pernicious; wherein infinite wisdom, power and love are precluded.

The philosopher or deist who could deduce the utility of a louse would be an object of greater curiosity than a woman sitting on seven hills.

To abide in the flesh is supremely sweet to all animates; thence how sad is the contemplation of the stubborn fact that the vast majority of animates, including man, maintain life in the flesh by subsisting on the flesh of others — by devouring the flesh of other animates, whose desire to abide therein is supreme, and yet who find their greatest joy in despoiling others of that which all esteem the greatest boon.

This one fact precludes the existence of a Supreme Being, infinite in love and wisdom.

Under existing environments, millions — yea, billions — of minds antagonize other billions.

This antagonism arises from different conditions of environment, wholly beyond the control of all animates. However, when mind becomes master of matter, antagonism will cease; all will have come to a knowledge of what constitutes true happiness, happiness being the sole aspiration of all. Man, through knowledge, will have attained to equal merits, equal possessions, equal rights; these constitute lasting and supreme happiness. Ere the consummation of these, the transgression should never be charged against the transgressor, strained of mercy.

"Let he that is without sin cast the first stone."

CHAPTER XXVIII.

SUMMARY.

IF truth is not a sure foundation for righteousness, alas for righteousness.

In summing up the foregoing to logical conclusions, we find the query is this : If God is spirit ; if spirit is life ; if life is that which manifests germination, animation and mind through matter ; if no one hath otherwise seen God ; if manifestations of life and mind are all the evidence we have of God ; if these manifestations give us a full, clear conception of the true God ; if Jesus and God are not one ; if God is infinitely greater than Jesus ; if Jesus is only a man ; if the world existed thousands of years before Jesus existed as a person ; if Jesus was not begotten by the Holy Ghost ; if the Holy Ghost is excarnated Jesus ; if Jesus never died ; if no one ever dies ; if life never dies ; if there is no death ; if Jesus was not buried ; if no one was ever buried ; if Samuel, Moses and Elias brought immortality to light thousands of years before Jesus departed the flesh ; if Jesus' flesh body was never resurrected ; if the flesh body of no one is ever resurrected ; if thousands in our day appear to their friends in flesh bodies, the very same as Jesus appeared to his friends ; if Adam's fall is a myth or fraud ; if there is no angry God ; if there is no hell ; if there is no Devil ; if there is no heaven ; if Jesus is alive in the aerial sphere, the very same as all others who have departed the flesh ; if there is no judgment seat ; if there is no white throne, — what, what must honest intelligent people think of those who believe, and persist in preaching, the villainous gospel of redemption of a few, by virtue of a vicarium, from eternal damnation inherited by all through Adam's fall ?

SUMMARY.

It is an axiom of morals, that everything false is pernicious in all its aspects and results.

In the medical profession there is some sense, science and honor; in the legal profession there is much knowledge and some honor; but the clerical profession is void of every redeeming quality, when working strictly within gospel lines.

The gospel *per se* is limited to a belief in the efficacy of Jesus' suffering and death to save man from inherited, eternal damnation.

When stripped of all extraneous glamor of morals, the gospel stands unique — hideously revolting, abhorrent in injustice and cruelty; it makes the innocent suffer for the imaginary guilt of others; it is a monument to dense ignorance; it was foolishness to the cultured Greeks and a stumbling-block to the bigoted Jews; it is a reproach to intelligence; and it is an unmitigated fraud, from the half-shekel as a sin-offering down to the crucified Jesus.

The shining virtues of good morals, cunningly intermingled with the gospel of vicari, alone has saved it, in theatrical parlance, from being damned from its inception — and all those who officiate at the altar, from Aaron down to the supreme buffoon blatherskite of Brooklyn.

Preaching of total depravity is the climax crime against man. It loads him down day and night with imaginary guilt, more disheartening, more grievous to be borne, than all other ills of life.

The time is coming when those who preach redemption of man from an inherited hell of endless torment, by vicarious atonement, in full for inherited guilt, and all crimes committed and omitted while in the flesh, will be hounded down as the worst villains on earth, and the vilest enemies of man.

Evolution of civilization demonstrates that honesty, industry and kindness fulfil all there is, or ever was, of law and gospel, and are amply sufficient to make everybody good and happy evermore. Meanwhile, Charity — in tears — suffereth all, endureth all, and raileth not.

PART II.

PHYSICAL PHENOMENA.

CHAPTER XXIX.

NEBULÆ.

We now invite attention to phenomena that are purely physical, wherein life or mind in any form is never manifested.

In consideration of nebulæ, we will try to arrive at conclusions logically deduced from premises established by the telescope, the spectroscope and the camera.

Nebulæ are possibly the first forms of all celestial bodies; but we shall not extend investigations to include suns.

Moses tells us that, in the beginning, the earth was without form. This possibly was his first and least harmful mistake.

The earth is constituted of matter; matter cannot exist without form. However, in the beginning, the earth was without globular form. Therefore our first inquiry is, What was the first form in which the earth existed, apart from matter in the aggregate and primal condition?

In interstellar space there are vast regions, embracing millions of square miles, and billions of miles distant from any sun or stars; wherein there is nothing but an extreme attenuated matter called ether.

This ether is wholly invisible. Its existence is only known theoretically, by results that would inevitably occur from its existence.

Again, in many of those vast interstellar spaces there exist immense fields of nebulous matter, so called, consisting of mist-like luminous atoms embracing millions of miles square.

The number of known nebulæ and star clusters had reached 9,369 at the beginning of 1895.

These nebulæ are either self-luminous or become luminous by reflecting the light of other luminaries.[1]

Nebulous — vaporous — matter could only have become visible when condensation had become sufficient to reflect its own luminosity or the light of some other luminary.

Space being unlimited, there is no occasion for crowding matter in any form.

It is computed by our ablest astronomers, that the nearest star is several trillions of miles distant, and that the distance from star to star is not less, excepting possibly in the binary systems.

Without matter, we could have no manifestation of gravity, but inasmuch as matter is unlimited in unlimited space, we have manifestations of gravity throughout space.

In those vast regions of interstellar space there are localities that may properly be called neutral places, wherein the attraction of surrounding suns counteracts each other's attractive energy.

Into such places matter dissipated from various celestial bodies of the universe drifts and remains, similar to drift matter that collects in large quantities in certain localities of the ocean where eddies form, as in the Sargasso Sea.

At this stage much patience may be exercised. Haste is not possible. Time is an important factor in the construction of worlds.

After æons of ages had rolled away, during which time this dissipated drift matter continued accumulating and condensing, at length became visible nebulous matter.

Eventually a condition arrives whereby this nebulous matter is capable of reflecting solar heat. The moment solar heat is reflected or radiated, the repose, the quiescent condition, of the nebulous field is destroyed, giving rise to motion, other than the motions arising from attraction and repulsion; whereby a change in the polarity of the atoms occurs.

In those vast nebulous fields it would be impossible for solar heat from any one sun to affect the whole mass simultaneously,

---

[1] The recent discovery of *cathode rays* may give a clue to the cause of luminous nebulæ.

the circumference of which is often millions of miles in extent. Neither would the central portions be first affected, nor yet the outer edge, but rather where solar radiation happened to be greatest, consequent upon greatest condensation.

It is plain that no neutral place in space could be formed except where three or more suns counteracted each other's influence.

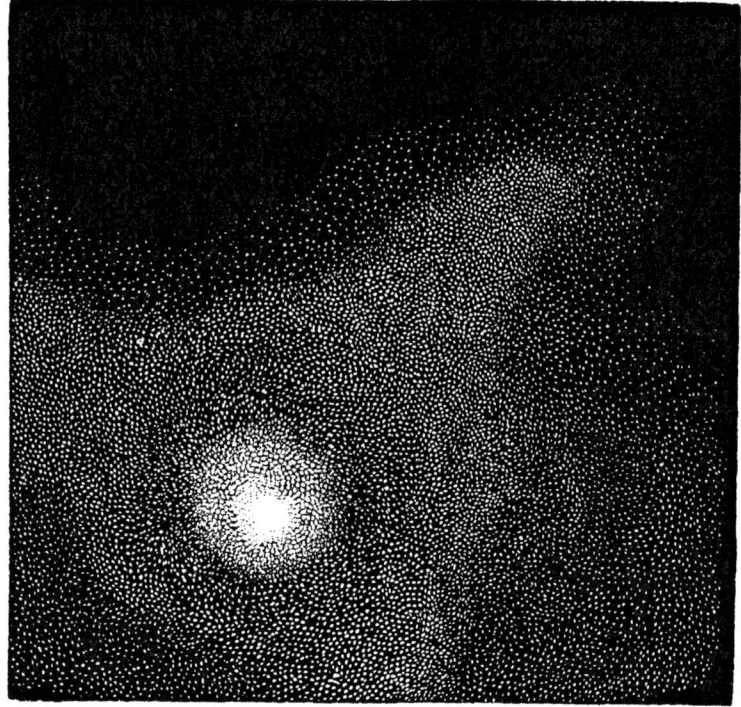

Fig. 1.

Consequently, nebulæ are only found in such localities.

And when such places become filled, so to speak, with nebulous matter, three or more suns dominate the mass, which is manifested by centres of commotion.

Logically, the first evidence of a sun dominating the field would be manifested by a bright spot, necessarily at a point where the radiation of solar heat was greatest. This is imperfectly represented by Fig. 1.

The gradual increase of solar heat would eventually cause a dispersion of atoms arising from their expansion, which necessitates motion. This is represented by Fig. 2.

Dispersion of atoms at any point implies the disturbance of the repose of the whole nebulous mass, and necessitates a crowding of the dispersed atoms, against adjoining atoms,

Fig. 2.

resulting in further condensation, which facilitates attraction, condensation and radiation.

Now as this initial motion arises from a disturbance of the equilibrium of the whole mass, consequent upon solar rays impinging upon some atoms more than upon others, it follows that motion, thus instituted, must continue and increase, both in velocity and area, and eventually become rotatory, consequent upon the unequal and one-sided effect of solar heat upon a limited area of the mass.

It is a demonstrable fact, that when solar rays impinge and penetrate upon motionless vaporous matter — a fog mass, for example — the upper edge of the fog, where the sun's rays first strike is thrown into commotion, which motion soon becomes rotatory. Thousands of small eddies are formed, each of which becomes slightly isolated from the motionless mass, and rotates in a convolute or spiral-like form until dissipated.

These eddies are variously seen, vertically or obliquely to the sun's rays, and become isolated from the motionless mass by ascension, until vanished by evaporation.

As previously stated, a neutral space could only be established where three suns — at least — counteracted each other's powers of attraction; and a nebula occupying said space would be dominated by these three suns, manifested by three bright spots.

It must be borne in mind, that nebulous matter is so attenuated that the power of attraction exerted thereon from any direction is better known by theory than otherwise. Bright spots in the nebulæ would manifest, prior to motion, thus showing that the thermal power in this case is more potent than attraction. Indeed, the thermal power always exceeds the power of attraction upon nebulæ; and, unlike the neutralizing effect of attraction upon the whole mass, these bright spots are only affected by the special suns that originated them.

Owing to the extreme tenuity of nebulæ, solar rays would penetrate the mass, millions of miles possibly, before the atoms would manifest their thermal power by brightness or motion.

For an illustration, let *a*, *b*, *c*, Fig. 3, represent three suns, distant several hundred million miles from the nebulous field.

If these three suns had the same magnitude, the central point of this neutral space would be equidistant from each sun; if unequal in magnitude, this neutral point would be where the attractive powers of these suns become equalized. Again if

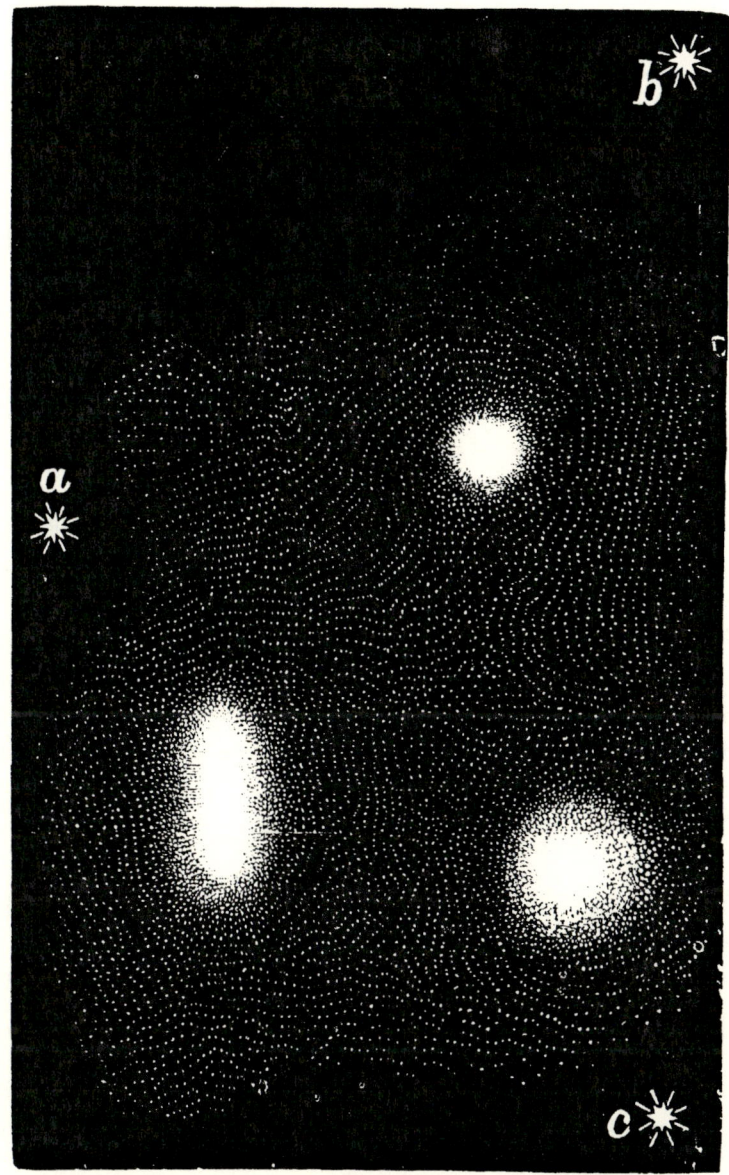

Fig. 3.

several other suns were to interject their influence upon the same nebula, although their influence might be too small to create bright spots of their own, they yet would aid or thwart the others to such an extent as to affix the spots a considerable distance from where they otherwise would have been.

It is plain that condensation would increase thermal radiation; and this, in turn, would increase the degree of disturbance of the nebulous mass, resulting in an increase of rotation. This increase of rotation, however, is not a result of contraction *per se*; but as contraction implies condensation, resulting in an increase of solar radiation and a greater disturbance of the equilibrium of the mass, it follows that an increase of rotation results from a concatenation of causes.

This increase of rotation, however, is limited.

When condensation has reached the limit where solar radiation is no longer increased thereby, then increase of rotation also ceases.

The earth's period of rotation has neither increased nor diminished perceptibly since Copernicus made the grand discovery of her rotation.

In course of time these bright spots, seen in Fig. 3, would manifest motion, volute in form, eventually becoming circular and rotatory.

The action of a sun's rays upon nebulous matter is exactly the same as upon aqueous vapor, so far as relates to motion.

Now, as soon as rotation becomes fairly established, a new motion appears, resulting from centrifugal force, generated by axial rotation, the energy of which is determined by the velocity of rotation.

This new motion is always in a direction so as to encircle the sun, by which axial rotation is created, and is the initial of orbital motion, as seen in Fig. 4, Sun *b*.

This rotating mass eventually becomes isolated from the motionless mass, and emerges therefrom in a cometary condition, drawing after it a considerable quantity of nebulous atoms.

These nebulous fields in space practically remain for aye. There ever remain vast bodies of nebulous matter, notwithstanding many comets may have originated therein and escaped therefrom.

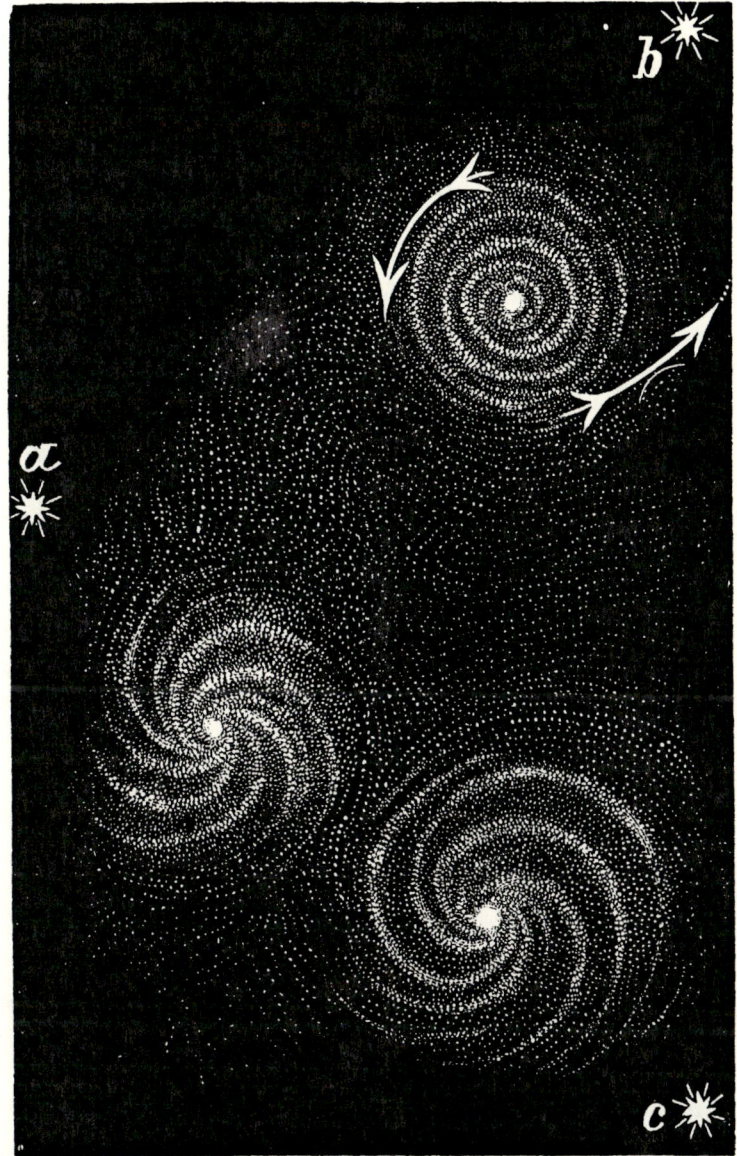

Fig. 4.

Those neutral places in space would remain in their exact relations to the same suns — as world-breeders — forever, were it not that all suns have orbital motion, although not all in the same direction nor with the same velocity; therefore, in time they lose their dominant power, and are superseded by other suns, whose motions have brought them into the dominant position relative to the nebulous field.

Thus every atom in the universe is constantly and slowly changing its relations to all other atoms.

Interstellar space is so near being a vacuum, owing to the tenuity of the ether matter that occupies it, that the resistance offered thereby to a body in motion is so very minute that but little energy of heat or attraction is required to impart motion to matter in this neutral region; and as the energy of attraction is exerted even in a vacuum, it is not strange that nebulous matter should follow in the wake of a comet recently escaped, chasing after it like a swarm of mist meteors. However, there are two classes of meteors, or meteorites. One class originates in nebulæ; the other, from disentegrating moons.

All satellites are slowly dissipating.

Owing to the extreme elongation of the orbits of comets, and the immense distance they travel, some are supposed to pass beyond the control of their parent sun — like boys who must go abroad to sow their oats.[1]

Logically, we should, if possible, follow comets from their origin to their destiny; but to do so here would anticipate a correlative subject which we wish to approach and discuss from another point of view.

However, we think there is but little doubt that comets become plain, staid planets, and eventually moons.

A comparison of several comets in various stages of development leads to this conclusion. The first manifestation of a comet is a bright spot in a nebulous field; the second is represented by Encke's comet, with smooth, fog-like envelope; the third is represented by Donati's comet, disporting a beautiful

---

[1] The paraboliform orbits of comets arise from their disk-like form, rather than globular. Owing to less cohesion of their particles, arising from their plastic and vaporous condition, the centrifugal force resulting from axial rotation moulds them into extreme oblate (disk-like) form; consequently, the centrifugal force is expended in lines that produce parabolic orbits.

tail; the fourth class is represented by the comet of 1585, the bright spot within the mottled surrounding clearly indicating a polar centre, and its whole appearance indicating axial rotation as a planet, while the sparkling, radiating rays indicate its cometary character. This comet is the nearest approach to the planetary stage of any yet discovered. Illustrated on page 175.

An immense amount of nonsense has been published relative to the construction and constitution of comets' tails.

Many scientists who rank high in scientific coteries insist that the tails of comets are composed of matter dispersed from the body of the comet by some peculiar repellent power, resident and emanating from the sun.

No force known to govern matter and motion warrants such an assertion.

The velocity of a comet, when passing in perihelion, is so great, and the length of some tails so immense, as to preclude the possibility of a vaporous substance sustaining sufficient velocity to whisk around the extremity of a tail — millions of miles in length — into the position required when the comet has again resumed its outward flight.

Light or thought is alone capable of so great a velocity.

For a full explanation of the philosophy of comet tails, the reader is referred to "Cosmology."

Prior to dismissing the subject of nebulæ, we wish to say a few words relative to what is known as the nebulous theory, or hypothesis, first suggested by Herschel, modified by Laplace, elaborated by G. H. Darwin, and largely believed in by many.

The basis of the theory rests on the *assumptions*, that suns originally were nebulous matter that filled space and possessed rotatory motion; that contraction of nebulous matter increased the velocity of rotation to such a degree that the centrifugal force generated by rotation threw off plastic masses that became planets; that contraction of the planets increased, which again increased the velocity of rotation, and in turn threw off plastic masses that became satellites.

Now, then, suns may or may not have originated from nebulous matter, but a nebulous sun has never been cognizable.

Again, there is no law in physics showing that contraction *per se* in any manner whatever originates or increases axial rotation.

Contraction, in obedience to the force of gravity, must be in a right line from all points of the circumference toward the centre of the mass. This is a law with no exceptions.

Professor Darwin's illustrated demonstration of this assumed fact (that contraction increases axial rotation) is ludicrously absurd, inasmuch as he substitutes *orbital revolution* for *axial rotation*.

In answer to the writer's queries on this subject a distinguished American astronomer states that, " As the particle nears the centre, it tends to preserve its original linear velocity, and as the same linear distance subtends a greater angle when nearer the centre, its angular velocity is increased."

Another distinguished American astronomer states that, " A planet contracting in equatorial diameter would have to revolve faster on its axis in order to conserve its original rotatory momentum."

Now it is plainly evident that the logic in both these statements rests on the silly assumptions that the rotatory motion of planets results from an arbitrary primitive impulse and moves in a non-resistant medium; and that this primitive energy continues undiminished.

The logic of sequences, however, shows that there must be a resistant medium; that a primitive impulse must diminish in energy; that the rotatory motor is a power exterior to the mass, is continuous in its action and constant in application; that contraction implies an increase of cohesion in the same ratio, and is an exemplification of the law of conservation of forces; that the energy of the attraction of gravity determines the degree of air pressure upon the surface; that air pressure as well as air motion determines the velocity of axial rotation. For example, Jupiter's energy of attraction gives an air pressure sufficient to rotate his great mass in less than one-third of the earth's diurnal period. However, this short period may be due in part to the more direct application of the rotatory power consequent upon the small inclination of Jupiter's axis.

Now, inasmuch as the energy of attraction determines the degree of cohesion and air pressure, while air pressure determines, to a great extent, the velocity of rotation, we here again find a correlation of forces that precludes the possibility of matter being thrown off by centrifugal force, unless the force arises from an arbitrary impulse.

Professor Darwin, in an elaborate paper, states that, about fifty millions of years since, the earth's diurnal period of rotation was only about one-seventh its present period; that, in consequence of her great velocity of rotation, the moon was thrown off, etc. However, it is generally conceded that the earth is constantly cooling; consequently, is constantly shrinking. Thence, if contraction increases velocity of rotation, why is the earth's period of rotation seven times longer than of yore?

CHAPTER XXX.

AIR PRESSURE, AND AIR MOTION, AS A MOTOR.

In our brief article on nebulæ it was shown how motion originated and became rotatory. We also stated that axial rotation created an orbital motor.

In order to clearly understand whence an orbital motor comes, how created, and how exerted, it is necessary to show the potency of air motion.

The earth is known to be surrounded by a vaporous ocean that is constantly in motion. This motion is wholly a result of sunshine upon half the earth's sphere and its absence on the opposite half.

Without sunshine, a death-like calm would pervade the whole earth.

Not a blade of grass would bend, nor a leaf tremble throughout the whole domain.

The radiation of solar heat from half the earth's sphere destroys the equilibrium of the whole aerial ocean, and thus creates motion throughout the whole vaporous body.

If the earth was as round and smooth as a billiard ball and all of the same material, air motion would be all in one direction. The whole circulation would be in the direction of the sun, otherwise called east.

But owing to the undulating and diversified surface of the earth — consisting of oceans, lakes, rivers, plains, mountains and valleys, each possessing different powers of radiation of solar heat — we find air currents diverge northward and southward, but never westward.

All the conditions that originally gave rise to vapor motion still exist, and are more potent than when the earth escaped from the nebulous field in a cometary stage.

When in the cometary condition, the matter therein was isolated, while rarer gases were intermingled therewith, whereby only a small percentage of centripetal attraction and radiation were possible, as compared with her present solidified condition.

When the earth was in the nebulous cometary stage, centripetal power was weak, consequent upon attraction not being exerted upon a definite centre; whereas at present the whole power is exerted upon one centre of the whole mass, with a potency to give an air pressure upon the mass equal to fifteen pounds to the square inch of surface, equal to 5,000,000,000,000,000 tons on the whole earth.

Now as this air ocean is in constant motion around the whole earth, in the direction of the sun, and is exerted around the whole circumference of the earth, in a continuous belt from pole to pole — exerted with a leverage power, at the equator, of 4,000 miles, its power as a rotatory motor is so enormous that the mind is wholly unable to grasp it.

The equipoise of planets in the ether of interstellar space is more perfect than the poise of a soap-bubble in air; and the more perfect the poise the more easily the poise is destroyed.

This perfect poise originally — as elsewhere shown — arises from the counter-attraction of several suns, together with the centripetal attraction resident in the mass; consequently there is not sufficient excess of attraction in any one direction to prevent or hinder an easy disturbance of the poise. And the moment the poise is disturbed, motion occurs in the direction in which the disturbing cause is exerted, which in this case is the direction of air motion around the mass.

Having thus shown the power that originates and perpetuates axial rotation, we are now prepared to show how an orbital revolution is created.

CHAPTER XXXI.

AIR, AND ORBITAL MOTIONS.

REFERRING to Fig. 5, representing a grindstone, it is seen that if water is poured on top of the stone, while at rest, all the water drips off in the line of *a*, in obedience to gravity.

If the stone is rotated with a moderate velocity, water will be thrown off in the line of *b*. If the velocity is increased, water will be thrown off in the line of *c*.

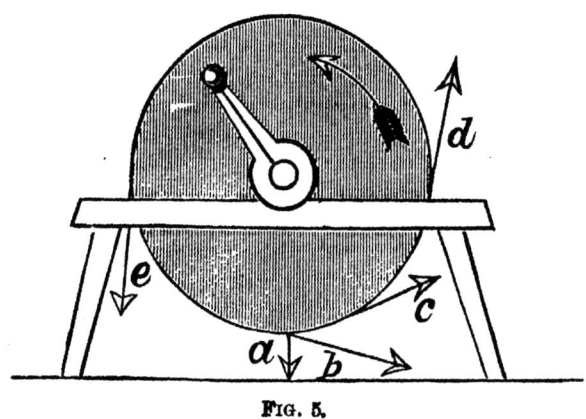

FIG. 5.

If the velocity is still further increased, water will be thrown off in the line of *d*, and with a greater increase, it will be thrown off in the line of *e*. All of which goes to show that various degrees of velocity change the points, quantities and directions in which the centrifugal force is expended.

The gyroscope demonstrates that centrifugal force, generated by axial rotation, with a given velocity, overcomes the force of gravity, and also develops a motor that actually produces orbital revolution. Consequently, the greatest amount of centrifugal force must be expended in the direction of orbital motion, inasmuch as no other power is found to impart orbital motion in any direction; furthermore, a proper degree of axial velocity is required to cause an excess of centrifugal energy to be expended at the requisite point to impart orbital motion in the proper direction.

The gyroscope further demonstrates that the greater the axial velocity the less the orbital velocity, and *vice versa*, down to the minimum velocity requisite to overcome the force of gravity.

The fact is verified by all the planets whose axial velocity is positively known.

Notwithstanding the gyroscope plainly reveals the foregoing facts, there is yet something of a puzzle in its application, as demonstrative of planetary motions, inasmuch as the gyroscope's axial and orbital motions seem to be in the reverse direction known to exist. We think this may arise from the fixed arbitrary centre causing the gyration in a line athwart the line of greatest attraction. However, we leave the solution to more able geometricians. Indeed, Professor Manning, in the *Scientific American*, gives an explanation going to show that the axial and orbital motions of the gyroscope coincide exactly with the axial and orbital motions of the earth.

The direction of the earth's axial rotation is ascertained by the sun's apparent motion westward and the moon's motion eastward.

To diurnal rotation of the earth *per se* is due all there is of beauty and happiness on earth. Without diurnal rotation the earth would be as desolate and dead as a moon.

But inasmuch as diurnal motion results from air pressure and air motion, all phenomena arising therefrom are not rosy hued, nor lovely to contemplate.

Floods, famines and tornadoes, with all their dire results, are caused directly by air motion.

Clouds are the results of sunshine; their transportation is by wind, also the result of sunshine. The fickle wind carries the clouds to and fro, causing floods in some places and dearths in others, and again tornadoes in other parts of the earth.

Now, in giving a logical explanation of these phenomena and others, our first statement is, that the normal circulation of the air is eastward, never westward under any conditions whatsoever. However, its direction may diverge northward and southward; but it always maintains a greater velocity eastward than in any other direction.

This fact is ascertained by the direction and velocity of clouds, as compared with the earth's rotation at the place of observation; the air really partakes of a compound motion when moving southward and northward. Furthermore, the normal circulation of air always crosses the line that divides the dark from the illuminated half of the earth's sphere at right angles. This line, for convenience, may properly be called the line of illumination.

Again, the normal circulation of air is always toward the sun, whether the sun is in his northern or southern declination of the equator. This is clearly proved by the change in the direction of the monsoons. For example, when the sun is at the northern tropic, the monsoons blow northeast; and when the sun is at the southern tropic, the monsoons blow southeast; and in each case these winds cross the line of illumination at right angles. Even as far north as the Aleutian Islands the winds follow the sun, same as the monsoons; while at the equator a calm exists.

Why a calm at the equator?

What constitutes a calm anywhere, at any time?

A calm can only exist when and where the earth's rotation and air motion have the same velocity in the same direction.

The equilibrium of temperature around the equator, resulting from the vertical rays of the sun, tends to retard air motion at the place where the earth's surface velocity is greatest; and thus the two motions are equalized, producing a calm.

AIR, AND ORBITAL MOTIONS.

When the sun declines north of the equator, this calm belt moves a little north of the equator; while a few miles north and south of this calm belt, the wind becomes tardy; that is, the wind's eastward motion is 23 miles less than the earth's velocity of rotation. Consequently, the winds appear to blow westward, and are known as the trade winds; but in reality these so-called trade winds have an eastward velocity of about 977 miles an hour.

All those winds that appear to blow westward, as indicated by low clouds, are surface currents, and arise from unequal radiation of solar heat, as previously explained, thus creating high and low air pressure in circumscribed areas. A low air pressure always retards the eastward motion of air that is immediately eastward of the low, and always accelerates the motion of air that is immediately west of the low.

This phenomena of tardy air currents is seen on both Jupiter and Saturn (Professors Hall and Williams).

In referring to Fig. 6, wherein the earth is represented in two positions and four locations, it is seen that at *a*, the earth is shown with her axis perpendicular to the plane of her orbit, moving in a true circular orbit in the line of *b*, while at *d*, she is at her vernal equinox, with her axis inclined 45° toward the plane of her orbit; consequently she is moving in an elliptical orbit. (All text-books teach that Venus' axis inclines 75°, as shown in the cut; and yet it is wholly impossible for an axis to exceed 45° inclination. We  hazard nothing in staking our whole theory on this one fact.) At *c* and *e* the earth is represented at her solstices, with her axis inclined same as at equinox *d*.

It is seen that in all these positions of the earth the air crosses the line of illumination at right angles, direct toward the sun; that when the earth is at either equinox, the air belt exerts its power in the exact line of rotation; but when the earth is at either solstice, the rotary motor (air belt) is exerted athwart the line of rotation forty-five degrees, represented by arrows *v* and *r*, and consequently exerts its power with equal potency to rotate the earth upon her polar diameter as upon her equatorial diameter. Notwithstanding the earth continues for a

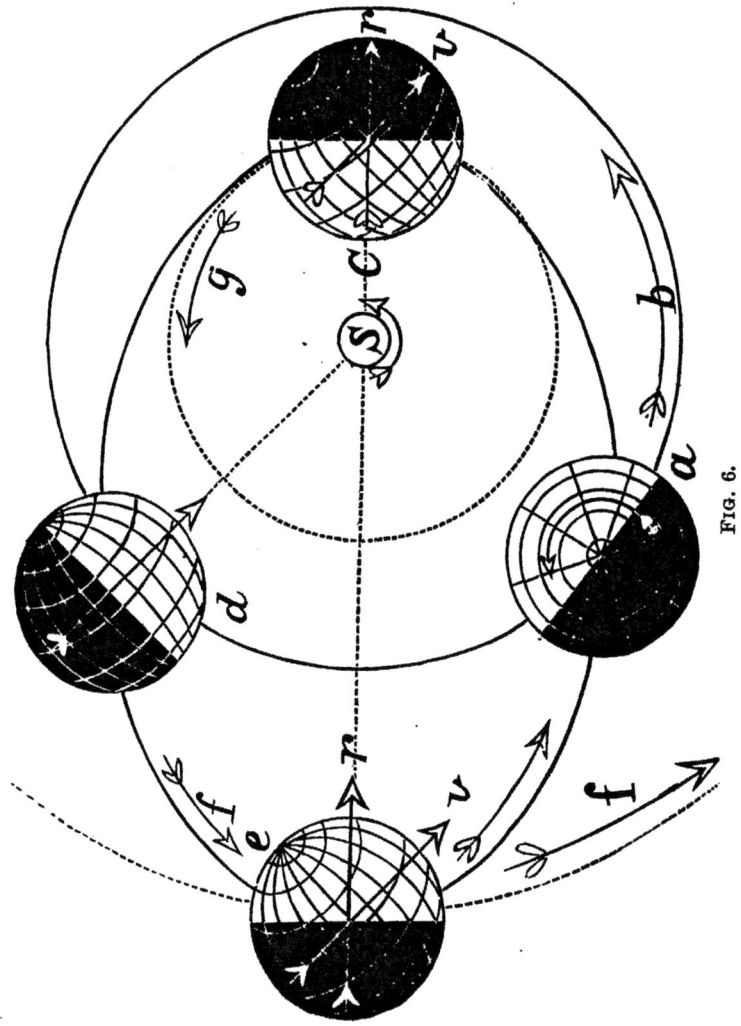

time to rotate on the old line, consequent upon the power of momentum acquired by rotation on this line. Bear in mind that this power of momentum remains the same in all parts of the orbit; whereas the power to thwart the old line of rotation increases as the earth moves from either equinox toward either solstice. Thus we find that while the old momentum remains the same in potency, the power to thwart rotation on the old line is doubled in potency when at either solstice.

Now, suppose that the blind, senseless energies resident in matter, known as gravity and heat, expressed by attraction and repulsion, should accidentally create a low air pressure 15° north of the air line r, and thus cause the air line to suddenly diverge 15° northward over a large area of the earth's surface, thus reducing the power to rotate on the line of the equator three-quarters; and, as a sequence, increasing the power to rotate on the polar diameter three-quarters; thereby the whole power to rotate would be exerted in the exact line of air motion. Under these conditions, rotation on the old line would cease, a new line would be created coincident with the line of air motion. The new axis would coincide with the line of illumination; the old poles would be removed 30° more or less, whereby the lines of rotation and air motion would be restored, almost or altogether, to their original and normal relations. If completely restored, the new axis would be perpendicular to the new plane of the new orbit; the new orbit would again become a true circular orbit. This reconstruction can only occur at or near one of the solstices. If reconstruction occurs at aphelion, the orbit becomes greatly enlarged (see arrows f and r); if at the perihelion, the new orbit becomes greatly reduced in size (see arrow g).

Now, inasmuch as the power to rotate the earth on her old axis exerts its maximum force when at the equinoxes, and its minimum force when at the solstices, the diurnal periods of Earth, Mars and Saturn may be less when at the equinoxes than when at the solstices. Again, we are told that the earth's poles "wabble a little." Now, if it is true, the wabble results from the unequal pull of the air belt upon the poles when at the solstices. Consequently, as inclination of the axis decreases, so will the "wabble" decrease.

A sudden displacement of the geographical positions of the

poles necessitates an immediate redistribution of the waters over the face of the whole earth.

The flow of water in any direction results wholly from gravity and centrifugal force, arising from axial rotation of the earth.

The changed direction of rotation arising from the sudden displacement of the axis of the poles, would cause the centrifugal force produced by axial rotation to act in concert with the attraction of gravity over the larger surface of the earth, and thus produce a flood that would deluge the greater part, if not the whole earth.

The rivers, lakes, and oceans that for thousands of years had been adjusted and distributed in conformity with the force created and expended by rotation on the old axis would now require to be readjusted and redistributed to conform with the new line of expenditure consequent upon the new line of rotation.

Old oceans would almost instantly well up, and leap over the rock barriers by which their proud waves had hitherto been stayed, and roll their angry waves over hills and plains, causing death and devastation over all the earth.

Chaos would reign again.

It is this sudden displacement of polar centres that terminates and creates geological periods.

When geologists accept this fact, they will understand the import of the emergences and submergences of large areas of land, about the cause of which there is, and has been, so much controversy and nonsense displayed.

The facts in geological, paleontological, ethnological and astronomical sciences, in proof of this theory, are so multitudinous that the writer despairs of making more than a meagre mention of a few of the more conspicuous.

Paleontology teaches that ocean denizens show gradual and continuous development from the lowest to the highest forms of marine life; "that a fossil of an extinct species of fish has never yet been found" (Professor Marsh)

On the contrary, land habitats show sudden terminations of types, and also abrupt appearances of new types.

"This sudden extinction of old terrestrial types and the sudden appearance of new types always occur at the end and beginning of geological periods" (Professors King and Marsh).

It is plain that when whole continents are submerged by adjoining oceans, marine creatures are transported with the waters to new ocean beds, and are thus preserved. On the contrary, terrestrial fauna and flora are destroyed by the element that saved the others.

And, as centuries roll on, the old ocean beds become clothed with verdure, and are eventually inhabited with new types of both fauna and flora — evolved, not created, in harmony with the climatic conditions by which they are environed. .

A displacement of polar centres to the extent of thirty degrees would cause the new tropics to overlap the old arctic regions, and the new arctic regions to overlap the old tropics; while two opposite sides of the earth would remain tropical during two geological periods in succession. On these garden spots tropical products would continue to flourish as of yore. Here, too, we find the interminable home of the colored man.

But in the new arctic regions (previously sub-tropical) ice formation would begin immediately.

Thus arctic winter burst upon long-haired, sub-tropical elephants, as they roamed and slept upon their hitherto congenial plains; but the pitiless snow and ice gathered around them fast and thick, and ere long they all slept in death. And they have remained ice preserved unto this day, silently but eloquently proclaiming the truth of the theory herein advanced.

In 1872 Captain Pavy and others, when exploring Wrangle Land, discovered what appeared to be whole herds of elephants imbedded in ice, upon which polar bears feasted and fattened.

As late as 1885, a long-haired, well-preserved elephant was exhumed from ice at the mouth of Lena River. Hereafter we shall see that this region had been sub-tropical.

We submit that nothing short of a sudden change in climate

could have produced and perpetuated such a strange and interesting phenomenon as this elephant in the ice; also, that nothing short of a sudden displacement of polar centres could have produced such a sudden change of climate.

Tropical fauna and flora are found underneath and on top of arctic fauna and flora, in nearly all parts of the earth.

The strata in which they are found are clearly defined, showing abrupt terminations and beginnings in every case.

In tracing out the logical results of a sudden displacement of polar centres, we find that every polar period has its ice-cap, its local glacial period.

At present, the earth enjoys two local ice-caps at her two poles.

The one great glacial period, so much talked of, is all a myth.

Dr. Hayes, of arctic fame, when in arctic regions marked a spot on ice. Upon his return, a few years later, he found that the ice had increased in thickness eleven inches each year. Hence in a few thousand years it will be thousands of feet thick.[1]

Now, although ice would immediately begin to form and accumulate at the new polar regions, the old ice at the old polar regions would not melt in a year or a century. Consequently, both old and new ice regions would exist at the same time.

Such large ice areas would reduce the temperature over a large part of the earth's surface, and thereby prolong the existence of the old ice-caps.

In 1869 we wrote and published that the topographical features, geological formations and saline deposits found in and around the Utah basin clearly indicated the location of an old polar centre in the basin. We also stated, in confirmation of the assertion, that glacial scratches would be found around the basin, but probably not within the basin, consequent upon the circumpolar ocean that always surrounds a polar centre.

[1] In a few hundred years the north circumpolar ocean will become filled with ice, over and upon which the pole may be reached with certainty and safety. North of the eightieth parallel, ice is already 6,000 feet thick.

At that time not one scratch of a glacier — to the writer's knowledge — had been found west of the Mississippi River.

However, a few years later, glacial markings were found all around the Utah basin — the Yosemite Valley had been filled with ice to the mountains' crest.

Later still, and better still:

In 1871, Clarence King discovered glaciers — ancient glaciers, living, but dying; mere remnants of glaciers that many ages since had filled the valleys.

Prof. John Muir has made a specialty of glaciers. Some fifteen years ago he reported sixty-five; and although some are miles long and wide, and many hundred feet thick, they are mere remnants. The conditions by which they were produced had long since passed away.

We are not aware that glaciers have been found southward of Utah; but northward, in California, Oregon and Washington, glaciers are numerous.

While in Alaska, where the old and new arctics almost or altogether blend, ancient glaciers of huge dimensions still exist. Near the coast there is an ice area 500 miles in extent, covered by a glacier more than 50 feet thick. In Glacier Bay the ice is 1,200 feet thick; and the markings clearly show that it had formerly been 3,000 feet thick (Professor Wright).

The gradual melting away of these ice areas is proof positive that they are not the creations of present arctic conditions, and must not be confounded with those huge modern glaciers gliding down from snow-clad mountain peaks.

However, the immense size of these ancient Alaskan glaciers may be due, in part, to their close proximity to the present arctic region, which has largely counteracted the thermal action of the Japanese stream (Kuro Siuro), the influence of which is felt and seen all along the Pacific coast.

These large and numerous ancient glaciers found northward of Utah have sometimes led us to think that possibly an old north polar centre might have been located northward of Utah; but the evidences of an old polar centre at and around

Utah basin are so strong that we yet hold on to the original claims.

Now, inasmuch as like causes produce like effects, we have abundant evidence that Lake Superior, too, once had the honor to preside over a polar centre, immediately preceding the Utah period.

Superior and Utah are much alike in their geological formations.

The rocks forming their basin all dip toward the centre.

The great ice-cap that once covered New England and New York more than one mile deep (Agassiz) was created by a polar centre, in the region of Superior.

The drift period, so called, resulted from the melting of this huge ice-cap consequent upon the sudden leap of the polar centre from Superior to Utah.

When Superior was a polar centre, New Mexico, Colorado, Arizona and Nevada were at least temperate zones — densely peopled, as evidenced by the many cities found in ruins, and the evident culture required to build them.

The ruins of Bonito, New Mexico, show a building covering an area of three acres, five stories high, with more than 800 rooms (Professor Bickford).

A temperate zone alone evolves culture.

When the pole escaped from Superior and became planted in Utah, these people were suddenly and unexpectedly caught by a pitiless arctic winter. Being unprepared for such a condition, in desperate emergency they walled up doors and windows, and thus remained. Many sought caves for protection, wherein they struggled to maintain life in the flesh; but in vain. All eventually perished.[1] So, too, the Esquimaux, from a like cause, will perish.

Great Salt Lake is near the centre of a basin 500 miles in circumference. Formerly the area of the lake was much larger. Constant evaporation decreased its area and increased its salt-

---

[1] If those people had known the true condition in which they were suddenly placed, they would have been masters of the situation, and moved southward — as indicated by the sun — immediately, and not have perished from earth.

ness; but of late years its saltness is decreasing, and it will eventually become fresh like Lake Superior, and filled with detritus.

This basin was once filled with a circumpolar ocean; within this basin, and also outside of it, in many places the plains are covered with saline deposits left *in situ* by evaporation.

Near Virginia City, in the dry bed of an old lake, salt is found, two and a half feet thick, of crystal purity.

It is well known that gold and silver are held in solution in sea-water.[1] It is believed that all the precious metals are so held.

It is also known, that terrestrial magnetism circulates from the equator towards the poles. The poles become magnetic, consequent upon friction thereat, arising from axial rotation; hence the magnetic needle points towards the poles.

The north and south polar centres are the true magnetic poles, notwithstanding the magnetic pole is at present near the arctic circle and near the 147th meridian, west longitude, Greenwich.

During the periods when the north pole was at Superior and Utah, those regions became surcharged with terrestrial magnetism, and yet retain much of it. Hence these old centres still hold in abeyance, to some extent, the terrestrial currents northward, and thereby prevent the magnetic currents from reaching the pole's present location.

But as the old centres are constantly losing their magnetism and the new centre constantly increasing its magnetism, eventually the new centre will gain the mastery; then the magnetic and geographic poles will be one.

Inasmuch as axial rotation is the cause and only source of terrestrial magnetism, it follows that the poles must eventually dominate and control the magnetism of their own creation.

It is further known that salt water facilitates the action of the voltaic battery; also, that ice breaks voltaic currents.

---

[1] About one grain of gold to a ton of water, held in solution by the iodide of calcium.

Now, then, terrestrial magnetism circulating from the equator to the poles concentres toward the poles; but owing to their encounter of ice barriers that surround the poles, the magnetic currents are broken before they reach the poles, resulting in the precipitation of metals held in solution by sea-water at the point where the currents are broken. Hence the vast quantities of metals found in the regions of Superior and Utah.

Superior will be found more abundantly rich in metals than Utah. We think Superior enjoyed a much longer polar period than Utah.

Near Ishpeming, Mich., gold mines are at present worked, of fabulous value. Silver, tin and copper are all found in the same region.[1]

In Minnesota, 20 miles west of Duluth, a large area of pure hematite iron ore exists, 58 feet thick.

It has long been known, that electro-magnetism hastens and increases vegetable and animal products.

The immense vegetable and animal productions in the regions of Utah are the result of magnetism in the soil, consequent upon an old polar centre in that region.

A castor-bean plant, near San Gabriel, Cal., has a girth of five feet; one limb has a girth of two feet. Ewes taken from the East have borne lambs three times a year; and two to three lambs each time. Professor Nooney informed me that he knew a man, twenty-eight years old, who grew six inches after he went to California; also, a horse, ten years old, that grew four inches after being taken to California from New Jersey.

Twenty-five years ago the writer published a prediction, that owing to this excess of magnetism in the soil, California would produce men of finest mind, and horses of fleetest foot, in the whole world.

This prediction has become true, in part, by Sunol's recent victory of $2.8\frac{1}{4}$.

[1] This was predicted and published by the writer in 1871. In the late '60's he tried, but failed, to organize a company in New York City to mine gold in Madagascar, believed to be abundant, consequent upon the existence of an old polar centre in that region. At that date, gold in Madagascar was unknown to the writer.

AIR, AND ORBITAL MOTIONS. 147

The necessity of a reconstruction of axis arises from the divergence of the line of rotation from the line of atmospheric motion.

Their normal relations are coincident.

Now, when the axis is inclined 45° *toward* the plane of the orbit, it is also inclined 45° *from* the plane of air motion. And to restore the axis to its original and normal position relative to these planes, it requires a polar displacement of 45° to bring all into harmony again.

However, the displacement of a polar centre 45° is hardly possible by one operation; for notwithstanding the rotatory power in this case is equally divided between the equatorial and polar diameters, and eventually arrests rotation on the old axis, still the momentum arising from rotation on the old axis is a power that would struggle with the rotatory force to maintain rotation on the old axis, which might result in the wabble of the axis into a position which would be an equal compromise on one-half of the whole distance, amounting to $22\frac{1}{2}°$, a decrease of axial inclination which would require a polar displacement of $22\frac{1}{2}$ geographical degrees.

Thus it is seen, that the distance a pole is transported at one leap gives a clew to the amount the axis is reduced in inclination by the operation.

The distance from Superior to Utah is about 18°; therefore, the axis decreased its inclination 18° while on its journey.

From 45° subtract 18°; this leaves 27° as the axial inclination when first planted in Utah. Hence it would only require a further increase of 18° before a new axis would be required.

The distance from Utah to the pole's present location is about 45°; but we have seen that it is hardly possible to transport a pole so great a distance by a single leap. Moreover, if it were possible, we yet know that the pole did not cover so great a distance at one bound, inasmuch as the present inclination of the axis is 23° 28′, and is decreasing its inclination half a second per year; whereas if the axis had cleared the whole distance by one effort, the axis would have become almost or altogether vertical to the plane of the orbit, and, as a sequence, would now be increasing its inclination.

Now, after mature consideration of the many contingencies arising, together with many phenomena existing, we are sensibly impressed and feel fully justified in locating another old polar centre in Alaskan regions; whereby we hope to explain phenomena that have hitherto been a perplexity.

If we locate a polar centre in Alaska, about 30° from Utah, and subtract this distance from 45° — the extreme degree of inclination — we get 15° as the inclination when the pole was first planted in Alaska.

Again, the distance from the Alaskan polar centre to the present polar centre is about 20°. Twenty degrees subtracted from 45°, gives 25° inclination for the new axis, when first planted in its present location, which is found to be almost the exact inclination of the earth's axis 2,348 years ago, when the last great deluge occurred.

When the north pole was located at Superior, Greenland was in the temperate zone. When at Utah, Greenland was subtropical. When at Alaska, Greenland became again temperate; and when transplanted to its present location, Greenland was yet green, but is now ice-land.

Thus, when the true trend of scientific research is obtained, everything is found in harmony therewith.

Laplace and others have expended much labor in figuring out the exact inclination of the earth's axis thousands of years ago; also the exact inclination it will have thousands of years hence; all of which has been based upon the visionary assumption that the solar system remains *statu quo*. Whereas change is the irrevocable law of matter throughout the universe. Several stars have disappeared within the historic period.

Jupiter's axis inclines only 3° 4', which is evidence of a comparatively recent reconstruction.

Mars' axis inclines 28° 52'; a divergence of the wind 15° from its normal course might compel a new axis to be formed any year.

Saturn's axis inclines 26° 50'; the great excess of his equatorial diameter, including his rings, over his polar diameter is such that we may not be surprised to see him capsize at any time.

The axial positions of Venus and Mercury are not known. But if Schiaparelli's conjecture be true, namely, that their axial rotation is the same as the moon's, then we know that their atmospheres have been dissipated, consequently are ripe for satellites, and only await favorable conjunctions with the earth to become her attendants; and there may be those yet in the flesh who will abide therein to see the earth honored with three moons. But we think Professor Schiaparelli is off.

Again, if Mars has but little more atmosphere than the moon — as per Professor Campbell — Mars, too, is ripe for a moon; consequently, Jupiter may soon glory in an additional satellite.

The logic of evolution shows that the time will come when mind shall rule matter; whereas the logic of facts hitherto shows, that the inherent energy of matter is yet master of both mind and matter.

As heretofore stated, metaphysical science teaches that friction *per se* is an impossibility; that every thought is suggested by previously existing phenomena; that all art is suggested by nature; that man is as truly a part of nature as the hills and valleys; thence we learn that all myth, all tradition, all folk-lore originated from facts. Exaggeration may have obscured or entirely hidden the facts — the phenomena — whence the myth originated; yet by logical retrospection the origin may be re-discovered. We have two modes of thought — two trains of reasoning — whereby such phenomenal facts may be re-established; for example, if we find energies resident in matter, the logical operations of which would produce certain phenomena, we may fairly conclude that such may have existed — did occur. Again, if we find existing facts — phenomena — no matter how remote, we are fully warranted in believing that similar phenomena may again occur, inasmuch as the inherent forces of matter are constant in action and irrevocable.

In Chinese literature there is a tradition of a great deluge that occurred in the seventieth year of the reign of Yao, about 2,293 years B. C.

The Noachian flood is said to have occurred about 2,348 years B. C.

These two deluges, described by different authors widely separated on the earth, were doubtless one and the same flood; the trifling difference of fifty-five years in data may fairly be accredited to error in chronology. The forces of matter in operation requisite to produce so great a deluge, could hardly be repeated in so short a period as fifty-five years; the cause of either or both, no doubt, was the displacement of the polar centres, elsewhere explained.

The descriptions given of the Noachian and Yao floods are not so different in the general narration as to justify the conclusion of two floods.

All are familiar with Moses' description of Noah's flood, and it need not be rehearsed.

In "Middle Kingdoms," by Williams, the Yao flood is described as follows: "The great and little islets; the inhabited places to their summits; the abodes of beasts and birds are now widely inundated for a long time. . . . I have forgotten my family. I repose on top of the Mountain Yoh-Lu." The description continues thus: "I offered a thanksgiving sacrifice at the solstice: my affliction has ceased. The confusion of Nature has disappeared."

From this description we gain a clew to the time of year at which the flood occurred, inasmuch as the thanksgiving sacrifice was made at or near the solstice.

Elsewhere we have shown that a sudden displacement of the polar centres would inevitably produce a deluge over the greater part of the earth's surface; also that displacement could only occur when the earth was at or near one of her solstices.

A Chinese divinity, named Newa, is credited with restoring nature to order again.

Another tradition gives the honor of "repairing the heavens" to a divinity named Yu, who is venerated as greater than Confucius.

The foregoing clearly shows that the great cataclysm described, was not simply an inundation of immense proportions, inasmuch as the heavens, as well as the earth, were in confusion. All nature was topsy-turvy.

We may remark that this confusion of nature could not have arisen from imagination.

Nothing less than reality could have given rise to such a tradition. But on the other hand, the repairing of the heavens by Newa or Yu was wholly imaginary — was on a par with Joshua's exploit of making the sun and moon stand still, and with Pope Calixtus' bull against the comet.

This species of fraud has been practised to deceive the people by every knave known to history.

But why this confusion of nature? In what form did the confusion manifest? Why the belief in the necessity of repairing the heavens? No matter how extensive the flood, the heavens could in no way be disarranged.

The sun's and the moon's position and path could not be changed by a deluge. All the stars would continue to shine as of yore, no matter how extensive the flood.

But suppose this great inundation was caused by the sudden displacement of the polar centres. Instantly the polar star would disappear, or be displaced 20° or more. Other stars and constellations would be in confusion. The sun and moon would disappear, at some places and in others would have their paths diverted 20° or more. No wonder the people were bewildered and crazed at the confusion of nature presented to their view.

Evidently the story told by Joshua of the sun and moon standing still, and Isaiah's story of the shadow on Ahaz's dial going backward, were traditional of this same phenomenon, produced by the changed position of the polar centres.

Yao reigned 105 years — 70 years before the flood, and 35 years after the flood. This, we may remark, is incidental evidence that the years prior to the flood were shorter than those after the flood, elsewhere explained, inasmuch as no other emperor has reigned so long since the great cataclysm.

Again, the Mexicans and Yucatans both have traditions of the sun falling.

The Mexicans date the falling of the sun 957 years B. C. The Yucatans date the falling 1,000 years B. C., a difference of 43 years.

Now, in what way is it possible to extract the germ of truth contained in this tradition?

According to the writer's theory of air pressure and motion, readjustment of the earth's axis becomes imperative when its inclination exceeds 45°; that readjustment must occur when the earth is at or near one of her solstices. Consequently a full and complete readjustment of axis would require a displacement of polar centres a distance of 45°, whereby the lines of axial rotation and air motion may again coincide as originally.

With an axial inclination of 45°, and the earth at her summer solstice, it would be all day on the 45th north parallel, for example, and all night on the 45th south parallel. A sudden displacement of 45° would equalize day and night to twelve hours each over all the earth; it would be the same in effect as if the equator had suddenly leaped northward 45°, whereby the sun again became vertical to the equator. The earth's motion being imperceptible, the sun and moon and every visible star would seem to plunge, not directly toward the earth, but southward 45°. See annexed diagram (Fig. 7), representing the earth in her summer solstice.

Now it does seem possible, and even probable, that on some portions of the earth the sun would seem to stand still, as related by Joshua; and again, at some other place that the shadow may have gone back, as related by Isaiah. But we have not yet been able to see or show that such would be the effect at places occupied by Joshua and Isaiah; and we think the solution next to impossible. If we knew the exact spot in celestial space where the north polar centre pointed prior to the last change, and the exact point in the orbit at which the change was effected, we then could tell the exact direction and distance the pole shifted its position. These data would enable us to tell on what portions of the earth's surface the sun would appear to stand still or plunge, and also where the shadow would go backward.

This field has been so meagrely explored that it is difficult to harmonize data and phenomena.

For example, we have seen that a discrepancy of fifty-five years exists in the data of the Yao and Noachian floods, and

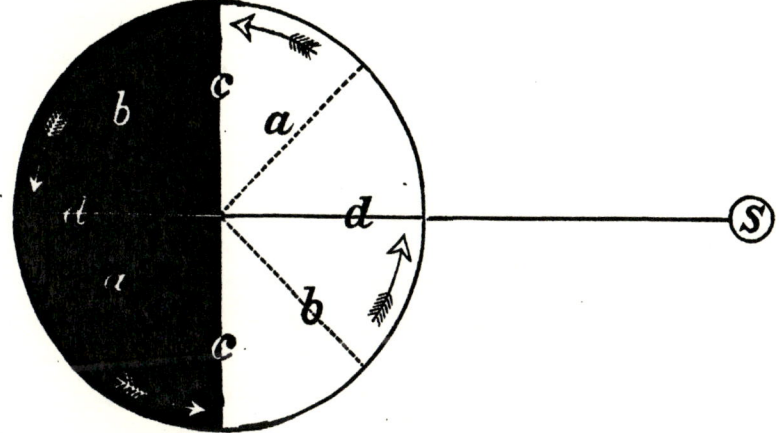

FIG. 7

a, a, old axis; *b, b,* old equator; *c, c,* new axis; *d, d,* new equator; *s,* sun at north tropic.

one of forty-three years in the data of the falling of the sun as recorded by Mexico and Yucatan; also, that an average of 2,684 years exists between the data of the two former floods and the data of the falling of the sun.

Professor Garczynski states, "that the old Mexican civilization had a more correct method of computing the solar year, dated from the falling of the sun, than our modern method." Now if this is true, we must credit them with considerable proficiency in chronology and astronomy.

In view of the foregoing data, the question arises, Have we had one, two, three, or four great cataclysms within historic periods? We hardly think so. Four deluges would give us four north polar centres; and notwithstanding we have located four north polar centres, including the present, and further think that Lake Tacoma shows evidence of being the fifth, or at least one of the four; yet we feel that several thousand years must have elapsed between each epoch, and that several hundred thousand years will roll away before another deluge can occur, inasmuch as the earth's axis is decreasing its inclination. And yet we know not at what moment something may happen in the solar system to arrest the decreasing inclination of axis and cause an increase.

Again, it is possible that floods may occur in the space of 50, 100 or 1,000 years. For example, suppose the earth's axis inclined 45°, which would demand a readjustment; and that when at or near one of her solstices, she made an effort, so to speak, of readjustment and failed, but succeeded to the extent of a few degrees. The sun would then seem to "stand still," or "go back" a little; the currents of rivers and oceans would be changed, and thus cause a considerable disturbance. The old forces continuing to be exerted, in a few years the axis inclination would again be increased so as to demand another effort at readjustment; thus several floods may have occurred within comparatively short geological periods, thus vindicating those several data herein given.

The Apostles in their day, like our lunar professor of Yale, were haunted with the fear of the world coming to an end, and, believing Jesus knew all things, inquired of him. The reply imputed to Jesus does him great injustice; otherwise, Jesus was wholly ignorant of the subject.

After giving a somewhat graphic description of the many signs and wonders that would precede the end of the world, he (Jesus) sums up with the sage advice, for those in Judæa to flee to the mountains, and for those on the housetop not to come down, while those in the field should make haste without even a coat. But woe to the women who were with child! Moreover, all should pray that this terrible day might not come in the winter, *nor on the Sabbath day;* for then there would be great tribulation. Here we plainly discover the earmarks of that gigantic fraud, the PRIEST. From all of which it is hinted that this great calamity was to be another deluge; else, why flee to the mountains of Judæa? But why flee anywhere? inasmuch as immediately afterward the sun and moon would be darkened and the stars would fall; and, to make bad worse, the Son of Man (which one is not stated) would appear in the clouds, with angels and horns — all of which would frighten to death those who had thought themselves safe in the mountains. And, as a last nail, he tells them that, verily, that generation shall not pass away till all these things should be fulfilled. This last declaration gives the whole thing away.

Nearly two thousand years have passed, and the end is not yet; nor any signs of it.

However, the sorest grief of all is, that bread is taken from the mouths of babes to feed an ignorant, pampered priesthood at a cost of fifty millions annually,[1] to preach such fraudulent, pernicious trash. Still it is not the part of wisdom to catch up the old refrain of, Woe, woe, woe, unto the inhabitants. Our consolation is, that *life never dies.*

It is not nearly so difficult to tell what makes the world move as to tell who among the many celebrities of the Old Testament is the biggest prevaricator.

Moses probably stands pre-eminent; however, as we have seen, Joshua and Isaiah loom up with great conspicuousness; while all three easily discount Sindbad.

Thence he who quotes Scripture in support of any theory runs much hazard of being worsted. Nevertheless, we venture a narration of Moses, wherein he states in substance, that God learned by experience that the perversity of man rendered it impracticable and unsafe for him to live six, eight or nine hundred years; so after due consideration, the Lord said, "My spirit shall not always strive with old men. Therefore, he shall live only one hundred and twenty years."

[1] Total amount, 1894, $87,901,655.

And to make his threat a success, he sent a flood and drowned the whole race, except a few choice specimens; and yet notwithstanding this wholesale destruction for the purpose of shortening man's days, Moses tells us, 661 years afterward, that Shem begat Arphaxad when he was one hundred years old, and died at the ripe old age of five hundred years; that Arphaxad begat Peleg at the age of thirty-five and died at the age of one hundred years. Then again, Nahor begat Tarah at the age of twenty-nine years, and died at the age of one hundred and nine; while Tarah — poor fellow! — died at the age of seventy, or fifty years before his time was up. Thus it requires six hundred years after the flood, to bring the boys down to the psalmist's threescore and ten.

Now, let us search for the grain of wheat in all this chaff.

The last reconstruction of the earth's axis occurred when she was at her aphelion, whereby she greatly enlarged her orbit, and, as a sequence, increased her orbital period; by which means, one hundred and twenty years after the flood was equal to several hundred years prior to the flood. There is not a shadow of doubt that the years were longer after the flood than before it; but it is exceedingly doubtful whether there was so great a difference as nine to one.

All text-books ludicrously teach that the air derives its motion from the earth's axial rotation; whereas the very reverse is true.

It is a well-known, demonstrable fact in physics, that the impact of a body in motion with a body at rest cannot impart to the body at rest a greater velocity of motion than its own velocity. Whereas the motion of the air, in the aggregate, is much greater than the rotatory velocity of the earth's surface, over which and around which the air moves; while in many places, covering large areas, the velocity of the air is often 300 miles, or more, an hour greater than the earth's velocity of rotation.

The motion of clouds clearly demonstrates that air motion is always eastward, and, as a rule, has a greater velocity than the earth's rotation.

Strange to state, this last fact is misapprehended by all of our *literati*.

An eminent professor of a technical college asked the writer if he did not know that the trade-winds always blew westward at the rate of 23 miles an hour. When replied to in the negative, he — the professor — laughed aloud; in which he was joined by all of his distinguished collaborators. However, when it was explained to him that the eastward velocity of the trade-winds was only 23 miles an hour less than the eastward velocity of the earth's rotation at that locality, it was easily seen that the actual eastward velocity of the trade-winds was about 977 miles an hour; whereupon he toned down considerably below the laughter octave.

In this connection we may be pardoned if we further state, that when a distinguished professor of one of the three oldest colleges on this continent was asked if he knew what made the earth rotate on her axis, replied, " O-h ! oh ! s-he s-h-e rotates herself." Again, when Professor Tyndall was asked the same question, he replied, " Oh! that is a big thing; Euclid himself could not tell."

For thirty years the writer has tried, but failed, to get one scientist of eminence to commit himself in writing for or against his theory. However, we may state that these so-called trade-winds are only surface currents that extend upward only a few hundred yards at most. Their tardy motion has a slight tendency to retard axial rotation : but these surface currents are impinged up on top by the great normal eastward current, moving in all its might and grandeur, which more than compensates for the small counter-effect of the surface currents.

Now, although the circulation is not always due east with the parallels of latitude, it is always eastward, and always crosses the line of illumination — the line that divides day and night — at right angles, except when made to diverge by local causes.

This fact is proved by the monsoons, as previously stated.

When the sun is north of the equator, the monsoons blow northeast of the parallels. When the sun is south of the equator, the monsoons blow southeast of the parallels. When the sun is vertical to the equator, the monsoons blow due east with the parallels; always, however, direct toward the sun; and in all these cases the monsoons cross the line of illumination at right angles. On the Aleutian Islands, where the winds blow unobstructed across the broad Pacific Ocean, they blow from the northwest during winter, and from the southwest during summer, crossing the line of illumination at right angles, the same as the equatorial monsoons.

Another most ludicrous misapprehension entertained and taught by all educational institutions is the assumed existence of what they are pleased to call polar currents, circulating from the equator to the poles.

This silly supposition is based upon the theory of the expansion of air by solar heat at the equator, and its condensation at the poles from cold, owing to the absence of solar heat.

Now, while it is a fact that heat rarefies — expands — air, and cold condenses it, the normal circulation of the atmosphere is in no way affected thereby.

The motion of warm air at the equator, and, indeed, on the face of the whole earth, is upward and eastward.

Those who advocate the existence of polar currents get their cue from the very limited swirl, or whirlwind, at the earth's surface, that never extends upward more than a few hundred feet. Without an item of evidence, they assume that this spiral ascending air is left-handed in one hemisphere and right-handed in the other, extending from the equator to the poles, and results from the earth's diurnal rotation; notwithstanding, no observer ever saw a spiral current extend 1,000 feet above the earth, nor a cloud 2,000 feet above the earth, going north. Moreover, the higher the clouds, the more calm and majestic is their motion eastward.

Again, the temperature of the air, at any given height, decreases as we recede from the equator toward the poles; and, inasmuch as cool air is more dense than warm air, consequently offers the greater resistance when both are unconfined, it follows that the bilateral pressure of cool air upon the intermediate warm stratum at and around the equator prevents the warm air from escaping toward the poles.

Furthermore, space area, relative to the earth (illustrated by the spokes of a wheel) increases so rapidly around the whole earth, while proceeding outward, together with the rapid decrease of temperature from the same cause, and the consequent condensation of air, by cooling as it ascends — all these, considered together, clearly show the impossibility of equatorial air circulating toward the poles. Thence, as before stated, no cloud or balloon, 3,000 yards high, was ever seen wafted poleward. Clouds are our only witnesses in proof of the direction of the wind. As elsewhere stated, all clouds move eastward as unerringly as the needle points toward the north pole. But owing to a low pressure northward or southward of a given locality, the clouds may, for a short distance and time, diverge north or south to within a few degrees of due north or south; but only for a hundred miles or so, until the low is reached and passed, when they again turn almost or altogether due east. All the while these same clouds had a much greater eastward velocity than in any other direction, ascertained by the comparative velocity of the earth's surface underneath them.

When a brush heap is burned, the heated air ascends vertically, while the cold air at the earth's surface concentrates inward from all points; and if a calm exists, a heated column of air rises vertically a hundred or more yards. If we could burn a brush heap all around the equator, the smoke would demonstrate which way the wind blew.

The writer regrets to state that he never found a learned professor of meteorology who understood what constituted a calm. All believe and teach that a calm results from a motionless atmosphere.

Prof. G. H. Darwin states, that a calm exists, "when as many molecules of air are going in one direction as in any other," all of which are invisible; whereas no calm ever did, or ever can, exist or occur except only when the air and earth have the same rotatory velocity in the same direction.[1]

It is a well-known law of physics, that the result of an impact is the same — the velocity being the same — whether the wind strikes an object on the earth's surface, or the object strikes the wind. It is further known, that a wind moving 300 miles an hour is terribly destructive, and that its force increases as the square of its velocity.

At Wallingford, Conn., August 9, 1878, a tornado, computed to move 300 miles an hour, "broke off stone monuments at their base like rotten twigs of wood."

May 20, 1891, a tornado passed near New Mexico, Mo., computed at 300 miles an hour, and devastated a path 300 yards wide; distance not known. In this case, an iron roller of 1,200 pounds was lifted up and dashed to pieces. A mowing-machine was carried 100 yards and torn to pieces. A horse was lifted, carried half a mile, and dashed to pulp. Many lives were destroyed.

Prof. C. Schaler Smith recently read a paper before the American Society of Civil Engineers, in which he stated that he had personally visited and examined the tracks of many violent storms, immediately after their occurrence, for the purpose of determining the force of the wind. He reports that the most violent storm recorded occurred at East St. Louis, Ill., in 1871, where the wind overthrew a locomotive. The minimum force required was 84.3 pounds to the square foot. At Marshfield, Mo., in 1880, a brick mansion was levelled to the ground; the force required was 58 pounds to the square foot.

"In all these cases, Professor Smith took the minimum force required, and considered this the maximum force of the wind, although the wind's force might have been much greater."

---

[1] Only a few weeks since, we read of a man on a Western train with a speed of 40 miles an hour — the wind having the same speed in the same direction, thus producing a calm — who was able to light his pipe on the rear end of the train.

Now, then, the rotatory velocity of the earth's surface at the equator is 1,000 miles an hour. At the 45th parallel, the velocity is about 500 miles an hour. The wind's force increases as the square of its velocity; consequently, if the wind at the 45th parallel would stop its eastward motion one second — the earth continuing its rotation — the impact of objects on the earth's surface against the wind would instantly manifest a force equal to a tornado with a velocity of 500 miles an hour. A velocity of 500 miles an hour would develop a force equal to 1,250 pounds per square foot (Professor Marvin).

A force so immense would not only overturn houses and locomotives and uproot trees, but would lift the oceans from their beds, would blow the tops off the hills and mountains, would in a few minutes reduce all to a general level. The mind is incapable of picturing the mad fury and chaos that would instantly reign over all the earth.

CHAPTER XXXII.

WATER MADE TO RUN UP HILL.

The earth's surface at the equator is thirteen miles farther from the earth's centre of gravity than the polar centres.

If axial rotation should cease, the waters at the equator would flow toward the poles until the centre of gravity became the centre of the earth's mass.

At the present time all large rivers divide at about the 60th parallel, north and south; those flowing north and south from this divide obey the law of gravity; those flowing toward the equator obey the law of centrifugal force.

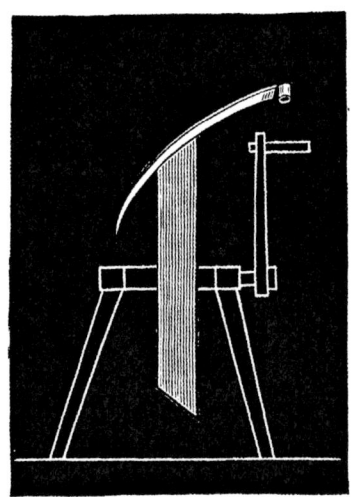

FIG. 8.

In the Atlantic and Pacific oceans, there exist the Gulf and Japan streams, flowing northward on the surface and southward at the bottom. The surface flow obeys the law of gravity, while the bottom flow obeys the law of centrifugal force.

This centrifugal force is not sufficient to make water run up hill, until about 30° from the poles.

We now venture an illustration and partial demonstration of this exceedingly interesting phenomenon, how and why water is made to run up a hill thirteen miles high.

By permissible digression, we state that when a boy of eight to ten summers, father owned the only grindstone in the neighborhood; on which all ground their axes and scythes. So much grinding soon wore the stone so small that a scythe had to be held on one edge, so as to not interfere with the long crank; and thus the stone soon became worn down to a bevel, as shown in Fig. 8, edge view. Being only a boy, I was subject to everybody's orders, and had much of the turning to do; during this it was noticed that the water was thrown off from the edge of the larger diameter. This was a puzzle; while

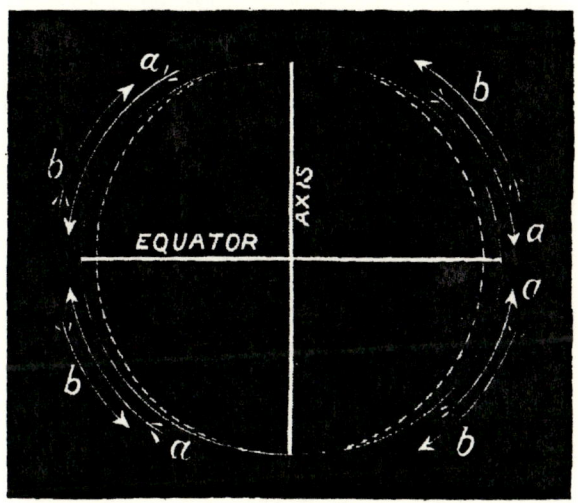

FIG. 9.

looking on the upper side it seemed as if the water had to run *up hill* to get there. I had never heard of centrifugal or centripetal force; but I knew something of up hill.

From this grindstone (bigger than an apple) I got my first lesson in natural philosophy, and now apply this small phenomenon, incidentally observed, to explain a similar phenomenon of huge dimensions.

Now, then, this bevelled stone represents half the earth's sphere. The edge of larger diameter represents the equator, Fig. 9; centrifugal force, created by axial rotation, forces the under current, shown by arrows *a*, toward the equator, up an ascending plane 4,000 miles long and 13 miles high. When the water has accumulated a volume at the equator too great to be sustained by the limited centrifugal force created by axial rotation, the top water flows back down toward the poles, in obedience to the law of gravity. Represented by arrows *b*.

This, we think, is a plain, logical solution of this most interesting phenomenon — a subject upon which much nonsense has been evolved by distinguished professors, fattened at the crib of our great universities.

CHAPTER XXXIII.

PHILOSOPHY OF CAÑONS: WHEN AND HOW FORMED.

"Constant drops wear rocks."

Cañons are deep, narrow water-courses, with perpendicular side walls of considerable height.

The Grand Cañon of Colorado has perpendicular walls of from 1,000 to 6,000 feet high (Powell).

Cañons are never found except in regions formerly occupied by polar ice-caps — polar glaciers, as contradistinguished from glaciers born of high altitudes, as on Alpine peaks or Mt. St. Elias. Glaciers resulting from altitude and latitude are not related.

Cañons are originally formed during the melting period of polar ice-caps.

One constant feature of glaciers is the existence of many cracks or fissures therein, extending from surface to bottom in a vertical line, notwithstanding the ice may be thousands of feet thick.

For illustration, suppose that Fig. 10 represents a vertical section of an ice-cap many thousand feet thick, filling valleys and toppling over hills; wherein a represents the ice-cap, b fissures in the ice, and c cañons cut down into the earth (d).

Thus it is seen that when the ice melts on the surface, the water pours down the fissures, a distance of one or more miles. So great a fall gives the water an immense wearing, eroding power; and as this constant pour-down through the same fissures continues hundreds of years, it is easily seen how fast and deep the groove in the earth eventually becomes, even when acting on solid rock.

The motion of an ice-cap is so slow and in one direction, that the width of a cañon would increase but little during the

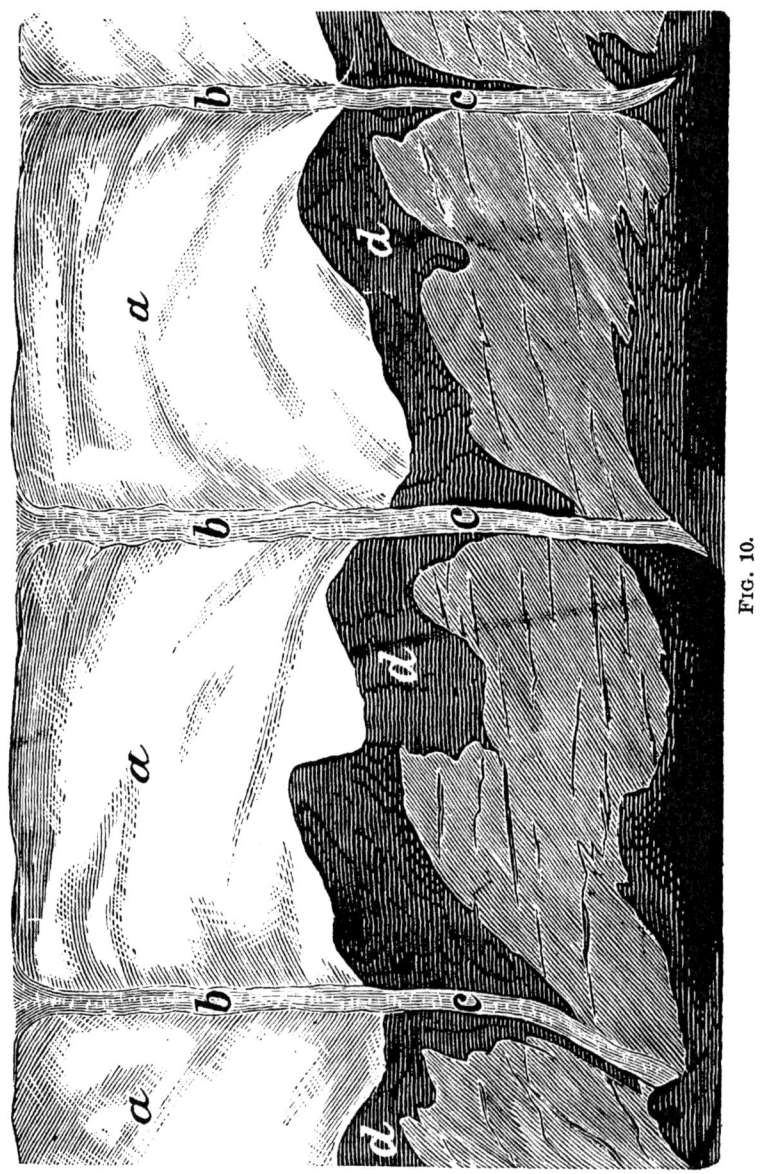

Fig. 10.

entire period. Indeed, polar ice-caps have no motion until isolated and confined to valleys.

When large areas, thousands of miles square, are covered with an ice-cap — not only filling the valleys, but also covering hill-tops — it has no motion; but when solution of continuity occurs thousands of feet thick on the hill-tops by melting, and the ice becomes confined in valleys, then the glacier partakes of motion in a line with the trend of the valley.

The constant and equal pressure of the ice on the earth's surface protects and prevents the sides of the cañon from crumbling; but many years after the glacier has disappeared, the perpendicular sides, if not solid rock, crumble and wash, and finally become narrow, ordinary valleys.

The Saguenay, St. Lawrence and Hudson rivers, ages agone, were grand cañons.

Indeed, the whole northern part of Pennsylvania, Ohio and New York States, shows evidence that every valley was once a cañon.

Now, in order to more fully comprehend the whole subject of cañon formation, let us once more return to first premises, and make a few logical deductions therefrom.

We have previously stated that nearly all our large rivers on both hemispheres drain toward the equator from about the 60th parallel, north and south; while those north and south of the 60th parallel drain toward the poles. It is well known that the earth is oblate at the poles, and very probably it is depressed so as to form a basin. Both Jupiter and Mars show a depression at the poles; at all events, we know that the present north polar centre is encircled by a circumpolar ocean 500 or more miles in diameter.

Now, then, if like causes produce like effects, it follows that a depression and circumpolar ocean must always exist around a polar centre, no matter where located.

The force generated by axial rotation of a semi-plastic mass always produces such a result; moreover, as the earth's crust is a mere shell compared to the earth's whole mass, it is clearly seen why the force generated by rotation causes a depression at the poles, and a bulge around the whole circumference of the equator to the extent of 13 miles of altitude; thus rendering the earth's surface at the equator 13 miles farther from the centre of gravity of the mass than the surface at the poles. Consequently, if the earth should stop rotation, the bulge at the equator might for a time remain; but the waters around and near the equator would immediately flow to the poles, forming an ocean six and one-half miles deep, around each pole, and thereby restoring the centre of gravity to the centre of the earth's mass.

Now, then, the centrifugal force generated by rotation is not sufficient to force water up the ascending plane toward the equator until the 60th parallel is reached; consequently, the waters north and south of the 60th parallel would flow toward the poles unless otherwise thwarted by mountain ranges.

It will be remembered that we have previously located old north polar centres in the regions of Superior, Utah and Alaska. A polar centre in the region of Lake Superior would give us a 60th parallel touching Mobile in the south, Hudson's Bay in the north, Nova Scotia in the east and Montana in the west. Consequently, within this radius, all the waters would flow toward the Lake Superior polar basin.

Now, what evidence have we that water ever flowed in the direction herein stated?

Prof. J. W. Spencer, after much labor and cost, has published a map showing that in pre-glacial times a large part of this area was drained by Lake Erie, which is a part of the Superior basin.

Prof. J. F. Crall has shown that the Alleghany River, in pre-glacial times, flowed north, and entered Lake Erie at Dunkirk; that Beaver, Shenango and Connoquenessing rivers all flowed into Lake Erie, in channels 200 or more feet below their present beds; moreover, that Lake Erie has filled up more than 200 feet since pre-glacial times. Now, if you will bear in mind that during the existence of the north polar centre in the region of Superior, all those great northern lakes constituted a circumpolar ocean, it is logically seen why those old river channels and the old polar basin have filled with detritus.

However, I would like to repeat in this connection a statement made in a previous article, that this pre-glacial prefix may easily mislead to illogical conclusions. Its misuse arises from the misapprehension that but one glacial epoch ever existed; whereas many of our ablest physicists believe that several have existed, under circumscribed limits. This, the reader will perceive, is in exact harmony with the theory of a sudden shifting of the poles' axis.

Furthermore, we must clearly distinguish between phenomena that occurred prior to, or during the formation and the disintegration of ice-caps; otherwise we shall misunderstand the logic of phenomenal facts.

If, during the Lake Superior polar period, a large part of the Northern States were drained into the polar basin, it follows that immediately upon the shifting of the pole's axis to the Utah basin, the immense ice-cap surrounding the old polar centre began to melt on the surface; fissures possibly had already opened from top to base; the surface water poured down these fissures, the ice being a mile or more thick; the eroding power of this immense waterfall, continuing for hundreds of years, formed cañons of great depth, exactly as now found in the polar region of Utah. However, owing to the long period since Superior was a polar region, as compared with Utah, the eroding action of water, frost and wind has almost obliterated their cañon characteristic; and yet geologists can still discern cañon formations. The old channels of Ohio, Beaver, Alleghany and Monongahela rivers are all filled several hundred feet, with drift deposits. The Ohio, at Cincinnati, is 200 feet above its old channel. Professor Wright found glacial scratches in Kentucky 500 feet above the present bed of the Ohio. Oil Creek, Pa., flows into the Alleghany 100 feet above its old bed.

In some places, the banks of the old channel are vertical (Professors Wright and Jillson), thus clearly showing their original cañon characteristic.

It must not be forgotten that all the foregoing evidences were obtained by those who were working upon misleading premises.

Once concede an old polar centre in the region of Superior, all becomes plain; and further evidences of the fact will accumulate so fast and abundant as to bewilder the enthusiast.

Now, inasmuch as a polar centre at Utah is only about 20° from Superior, it is possible that the Superior basin continued to drain all the Northern portion of the States for thousands of years, until the pole was again shifted to Alaska, or to its present position.

The central portion of Alaska is 40° from Superior; this distance would give centrifugal energy sufficient to change the flow of water from the basin toward the equator. Meanwhile, the Superior basin had been gradually filling up with detritus, and thus aided the flow in the direction of the equator.

A careful and thorough exploration of the beds of those great fresh-water lakes will discover that, during the Superior period, all those lakes were salt water; saline deposits will be found beneath their present beds.[1]

The shifting of the pole westward from Superior indicates that the leap occurred when the earth was at or near her summer solstice; that when the pole was shifted from Utah to Alaska, the earth was at or near her winter solstice; that when the earth was shifted to its present position, the earth had passed her summer solstice.

It is well known to geologists that the old channel of the great Susquehanna River is traceable the entire length of Chesapeake Bay, some 200 or more miles; that this old channel is fairly in the centre of the Bay; and that it is of great depth, as compared with the shallow water on each side. Owing to the flood and ebb tides, the old channel has filled but little with diluvium. The question is, Why is 200 miles of

---

[1] And yet, it is possible that the Superior polar centre was located so far inland that the ocean never reached the centre; that those great lakes resulted from the melting of polar ice two miles thick.

this old channel now submerged by this arm of the sea? Why did old ocean back up, as it were, the Susquehanna valley 200 or more miles, and thereby obliterate the river the whole distance? Delaware and Hudson rivers both show evidence of submergence. If we concede that the north pole long ago was located in the Lake Superior region, during which period the Susquehanna flowed as now, but extended 200 miles farther before it reached the ocean, all becomes plain.

Bearing in mind that centrifugal energy created by axial rotation is the force that causes the undercurrent in the Atlantic Ocean to flow toward the equator, and causes the water to accumulate there (elsewhere explained), it is plainly seen, that when the north pole became located in its present position, about 40° north of Superior, the equator was also removed 40° North, nearly 3,000 miles northward. Consequently, the excess of water that had accumulated at the equator must of necessity flow back northward to the new equator; and thus old ocean was forced to extend his shores northward, submerging the Susquehanna valley 200 or more miles.

Notwithstanding the abundance of evidence existing in proof of the foregoing theory of natural phenomena, much of which is clearly demonstrative, the author despairs of converting old men to a belief in so radical an innovation of old ideas. All hope rests with the young men of the rising generation.

Daniel Copernicus yearned in *vain* for recognition of his grand system before he departed this life.

CHAPTER XXXIV.

GLACIAL PHENOMENA.

GLACIAL phenomena constitute by far the greatest wonder and perplexity of scientists throughout the world.

For more than half a century scientists have been striving to find an adequate cause for the enormous ice-caps that have covered large areas in Europe and America, and also a reason for their dispersion. Professor Agassiz spent the better part of his active life in search of glacier scratches. Professor Muir has spent twenty years in search of ancient glaciers. Professor Wright has explored Europe and America for data wherewith to discover the cause of glaciation. His great work, "Ice Age in North America," is an enduring monument to his indefatigable labors and candor. Notwithstanding the many conjectural hypotheses that have been conjured up, all have proved inadequate to explain the primal cause of glaciation.

The hypotheses that have received the greatest and most favorable consideration are what is known as the astronomical and geological.

The first is based upon the variation of the sun's eccentricity relative to the earth during her orbital revolutions; whereby frigidity of the hemispheres alternately occurs: and yet all know that the annual amount of heat received by the earth from the sun on both her hemispheres is absolutely the same, without regard to the degree of eccentricity.

The geological hypothesis is based upon the assumed change of land levels, and the further assumption that high altitude is a prerequisite to glaciation. This hypothesis seems wholly untenable. When we consider the rapidly increased resistance of water as we descend to greater depths, we gain a fair knowledge of the immense resistance of the earth's molten interior to the exterior crust. We thus learn how impossible it is for the earth's crust to subside, which, at most, is a mere shell as compared with the interior mass. The apparent submergence of large areas is not conclusive evidence. Nor are our great mountain ranges conclusive evidence of their upheaval. Upheaval implies force exerted from beneath.

Mountain ranges are evidently only bulges on the earth's crust, consequent upon shrinkage of the interior mass; whereby the earth's *hide* is made to wrinkle, producing corrugations on the surface. Many of the smaller hills and valleys result from erosion by weather and water. In moderately high altitudes the velocity of water currents excavates valleys. In lower altitudes, owing to more sluggish currents, plains are produced by wash of material from higher altitudes. True, we have small areas of elevations by volcanic action; but nowhere do we find subsidence *per se* of large areas.

Tide water being our base line of altitude, when we find coast lines receding from land or advancing upon it, it is poor logic to assume that the land is either rising or sinking — having in mind the constant and inexorable force of gravity and the immense interior resistance.

Now, if it is a fact — which we are not prepared to dispute — that coast lines are receding in some places and advancing in others, it seems possible that the cause arises from a gradual shifting of the poles geographically.

We know of no cosmic force to prevent such an occurrence. Again, if the earth's axis is decreasing its inclination, it is possible that the poles shift to that extent annually.

However, if gradual shifting of the poles were the only mode of displacement, uniformity and continuity of geological formations would be found all over and all through the earth's crust; but inasmuch as geological strata show abrupt terminations and

174   PHILOSOPHY OF PHENOMENA.

beginnings of periods, it follows that gradual shifting of the poles fails to explain existing phenomena.

Therefore, in view of the present status of the subject, we deem it advisable to devote a chapter to the elucidation of the great phenomenon of glaciation. A full explanation requires us to revert to foundation principles, found in meteorological science. If we can establish our basis upon meteorological phenomena, then we have fair wind, full sails and beautiful waters.

INCEPTION OF GLACIATION.

From the time the earth rolled out her first orbital revolution she enjoyed an axis of rotation; the axis was perpendicular to the plane of the new orbit; and the orbit was a true circle, except slight perturbations as seen in the moon's orbit.

Immediately upon the initiation of axial rotation, the earth's mass became globular in form; but owing to its great plasticity at this infantile period, the bulge at the equator greatly exceeded its present bulge. As a sequence, the earth was more oblate at the poles than at present; consequently, while the sun's rays then, as now, struck the equator vertically, those rays that reached the poles impinged thereon in a line almost parallel with the horizon. In such a case but little solar heat would be felt at the poles; therefore the moment the earth's crust became solidified at the poles sufficient to prevent the escape of interior heat, congelation began, notwithstanding the great depression at the poles. But at this early period the poles would be the last to incrust over. Long ages rolled away before the crust became cooled and solidified around the poles.

In Fig. 11, representing the comet (so-called) of 1585, we have a beautiful illustration of a planet in this stage, wherein the crust is partly cooled; through which gleams of the molten interior sparkle. The dark and bright elongations of the molten crust clearly indicate axial rotation; while the polar centre shows bright scintillations of light radiating therefrom across the mottled body, thus giving irrefutable evidence of the existence at that period of that much ridiculed idea known as Symm's hole.

Inasmuch as the truth of our theory of glaciation rests wholly upon whether it is a *fact* or a *delusion* that the earth's diurnal motion results from air pressure and air motion, it is proper to again explain the *modus operandi*.

We may state that our first idea of the cause of diurnal rotation seized us July 4, 1849, and has never ceased to haunt us. Meanwhile its evolution has exceeded our wildest dreams.

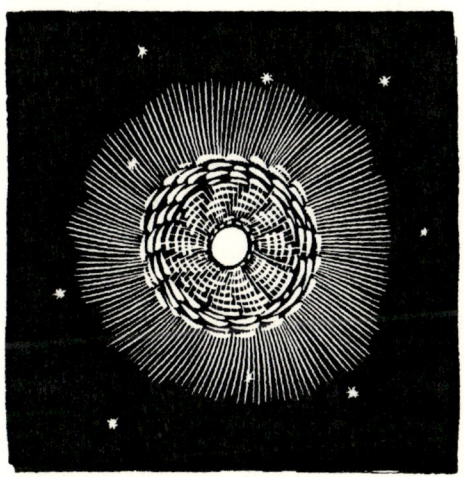

FIG. 11.

Now suppose, for example, that we poise a globe one foot in diameter in mid-air, and inclose it in an envelope that exerts one pound of pressure upon every square inch of surface; now, if the envelope is made to revolve in any direction, surely the globe will revolve in the same direction with the envelope. Again, if we inclose a globe one hundred feet in diameter in an envelope exerting one pound of pressure upon every square inch of surface, the result will be the same. Notwithstanding, in the latter case, the mass has greatly increased in ratio over and above the increase of diameter, yet we have, as an offset, a greatly increased superficies, together with an increased leverage, through which the energy of pressure is exerted, thus producing the same result as in the first example.

Bear in mind that the poise of a large body is as perfect as the poise of a small body; therefore, owing to the greater leverage through which the disturbing force is exerted from the circumference, it is seen that the poise of a large body is the more easily disturbed — that the poise of Jupiter is more easily disturbed than the poise of the earth. All planets are virtually in a state of equipoise, consequent upon the force of gravity converging in right lines from all points of the circumference toward a common centre; whereby the whole force of gravity becomes neutralized relative to the whole mass.[1]

Now while the earth is virtually in a state of equipoise in space, yet if she should stop her motion, she would undoubtedly fall to the sun; but she would not be in great haste to do so. However, her centrifugal force arising from her orbital revolution is not so great a factor in preventing her from falling to the sun as the centrifugal force arising from her axial rotation, as elsewhere shown.

But while the earth is, and remains, in a state of equilibrium, the aerial ocean by which she is enveloped never was, nor indeed ever can be, in a state of equilibrium, as elsewhere shown.

Now then, this aerial envelope of the earth exerts 15 pounds of pressure upon every square inch of globe surface, through a leverage of 4,000 miles; hence this globe of 8,000 miles diameter must revolve in the same direction in which her envelope is made to revolve. If we further extend this logic to Jupiter, we have a globe 90,000 miles in diameter inclosed in an envelope that exerts more than thirty pounds of pressure to every square inch of his surface, through a leverage of 45,000 miles. Hence, owing to his greater pressure and greater leverage, we find, as evidence of a greater potency of the envelope, the fact that Jupiter's diurnal period is only

---

[1] Originally the earth existed as a nebulous cloud poised in space. Her evolution to the globular form, and axial and orbital motions, in no way affected her original equipoise.

seven hours; whereas the earth's diurnal period is twenty-four hours.

It is no plea to say, that, owing to the vaporous and gaseous condition of the atmosphere, it has no analogy to a solid envelope, and consequently has no pull on the earth's surface.

It is well known that when the wind's velocity exceeds the earth's velocity of rotation by 75 or 100 miles an hour, great trees are bent and swayed and torn up by the roots, thus manifesting an immense force, exerted in the exact line in which rotation is found.

Again, when we consider the huge, rolling, dashing and lashing ocean waves, covering three-fourths of the earth's surface, we gain a fair knowledge of the mighty energy of this untamed, invisible giant.

Moreover, the wind's velocity ofttimes exceeds the earth's velocity by 300 miles an hour; at which speed it exerts a horizontal pull upont he earth's surface equal to 84 pounds to the square foot, and exerted with a leverage of 4,000 miles upon a globe perfectly poised by force of gravity.

It must be evident to logical minds, that a globe of any given size, when inclosed within an envelope that exerts a pressure upon every square inch of globe surface, is completely isolated from every other disturbing influence; therefore, of necessity, it is wholly under the control of the inclosing envelope, whether the envelope is gaseous, aqueous or solid.[1]

Surely, we have heretofore shown that the great normal circulation of the air is eastward, always eastward; that it has an average velocity greater than the earth's velocity of rotation; and that those tardy currents of wind that seem to blow westward, are only surface currents of comparatively small areas. On top of Mount Teneriffe, 12,173 feet above the sea, and on top of Mauna Loa, 6,000 feet above the sea, the wind

---

[1] It is evident to the least philosophical mind that any substance capable of *exerting pressure* upon an adjoining substance must necessarily create *friction* with the adjoining substance when either is in motion. A frictionless *substance* is unknown.

178   PHILOSOPHY OF PHENOMENA.

blows from the west toward the east, every hour in the year, with a greater speed than the earth's velocity of rotation (Tyndall).

It would be safe to offer $100,000 for the discovery of an east wind anywhere on the face of the whole earth, except possibly at or near the poles, where much confusion of currents exists.

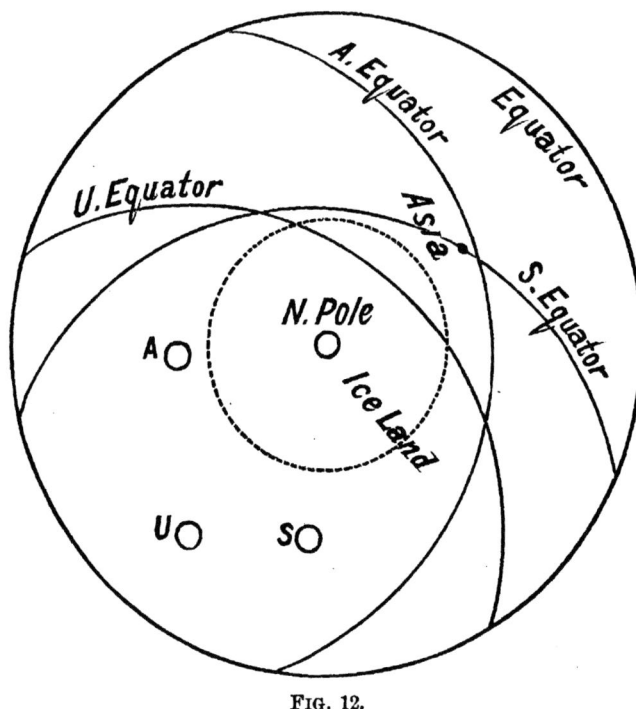

FIG. 12.

Now, if the reader will concede that we have fairly established the premises concerning our theory as to how diurnal rotation originated and is perpetuated, and will kindly turn to page 147, wherein it is shown how air pressure and air motion shift polar centres 25° more or less, we will next invite his attention to Fig. 12, representing a vertical view of the northern hemisphere, wherein we have located four north polar centres, namely, at Lake Superior, Salt Lake (Utah) and Alaska, and including the present position of the pole.

Now, assuming that the Superior polar period preceded the Utah period, that the Utah period preceded the Alaska period, that the Alaska period preceded the present period, we thence learn that every period creates a new orbit in shape, area and plane — a new horizon, a new equatorial line and new zones.

When the north pole was at Superior, or somewhere in that region, the equator was 40° south of its present position; and, as a sequence, the Hudson, Delaware and Susquehanna rivers extended southward several hundred miles before they reached the ocean. Greenland was in the temperate zone; the region of Utah was sub-tropical. When the pole leaped from Superior to Utah, that region suddenly became frigid; Greenland became sub-tropical. Meanwhile, the immense ice-cap, two miles or more thick, that had accumulated around Superior, extending southward to Manhattan Island, stood as a barrier to prevent the ocean from following up the pole to its normal coast line in that region. But after hundreds of years had registered, and the ice barrier had been removed by melting, tide water moved northward. Again, when the pole was suddenly shifted to Alaska, Superior became sub-tropical; and if the ice had not already disappeared from Superior, the floods would have been immense. Meantime, Utah became temperate, and her ice began to disappear rapidly, giving rise to terrific floods. During all these three periods, Northern Asia was tropical, as shown in the illustration.

After the pole became planted in its present position, Greenland became ice-land, and is already capped with ice 6,000 feet thick, which is increasing eleven inches annually (Hayes), and will continue to increase in thickness and area, while the pole remains in its present position.

Inasmuch as the earth's axis is decreasing its inclination, and inasmuch as a greatly increased inclination must occur before a readjustment is required, it is highly probable that several hundred thousand years will pass away before the earth passes through another cataclysm; and yet, if one or more sister planets should shift their polar centres, the present polar period

180   PHILOSOPHY OF PHENOMENA.

may be greatly shortened. Meanwhile, remnants of old polar ice-caps linger in Utah and Alaska, thus demonstrating the pre-glacial conditions of both regions.

It may be mentioned, that, during the Alaskan period, coast lines in the east moved northward up the Hudson; but when the pole was shifted to its present position, coast lines receded again southward, in accordance with laws heretofore explained.

Furthermore, as each polar period creates its own horizon, it

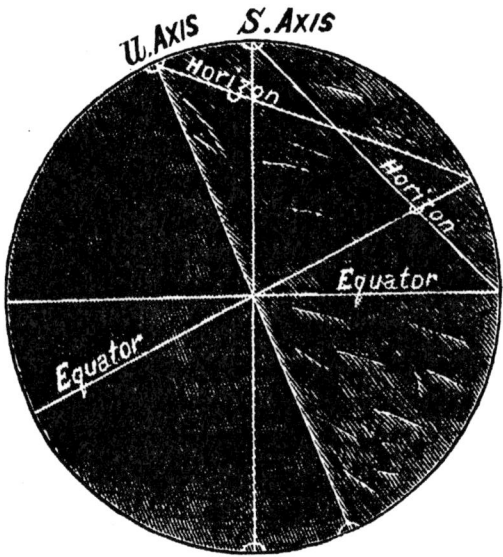

Fig. 13.

is seen that rocks laid down by aqueous agency would be parallel with the plane of the horizon of the period; but when the poles had shifted 20° or more, these same rocks would show a dip to the same extent the pole had shifted its position; and yet the rocks had remained undisturbed. (See Fig. 13, in which *S* represents the Superior axis, and *U* the Utah axis.)

It will be noted that no attempt has been made to locate south polar centres, nor to locate a north polar centre prior to the Superior period.

The discovery and location of those most interesting duplicates is purposely left for others, as an expert balance sheet, to prove or disprove this theory. However, it may be suggested that gold and silver deposits will be the leading factors of success in the discovery of south polar centres.[1]

It is not assumed that the writer is familiar with details of local phenomena. If the foregoing explains the perilous changes through which our dear old earth has struggled, he is more than paid for the toil of nearly half a century.

---

[1] GOLD IN THE TRANSVAAL. — London, January 6th. The gold fields of Transvaal are 45 miles long and three to five wide. They have been drilled 5,000 feet, and grow richer with depth. The mines will produce $13,000,000 per month, and there is $50,000,000,000 worth of gold in sight. John B. Robinson, one of the mine owners, is the richest man in the world. His wealth is estimated at $350,000,000, which he has made since 1878. His annual income is $25,000,000. He has one diamond which weighs 971 carats, and for which he was offered $1,250,000.

CHAPTER XXXV.

MOONS AND THEIR MOTIONS.

IF air pressure and air motion on the surface of planets originate and perpetuate axial rotation of planets, it follows that celestial bodies without an atmosphere can have no axial rotation *per se*.

It is conceded that our moon has but little, if any, atmosphere whatever; therefore it can have no axial rotation.

Now we think this logic fairly good; and yet, strange to tell, all text-books teach that the moon rotates once on her own axis during each orbital revolution. In proof of which they refer to the fact that the moon always presents the same side to the earth.

A contradiction of this silly logic is sure to elicit an angry disputation from all classically educated. Therefore, we venture an illustrated demonstration to show the fallacy of this scientific bosh.

In Fig. 14, let e represent the earth, m the moon, and s a spear thrust through the moon, transfixing the poor man in the moon, while the handle is held by some distinguished astronomer resident on earth.

Now, when the moon makes one orbital revolution, it is plain that the same side is always presented to the earth; and it is equally plain that the moon could not possibly have rotated once on her own axis with the spear affixed and held by an astronomer standing on earth.

However, the moon did turn once on her own orbital centre, and that is why she presents the same side to the earth. The difference is very material; it is as wide as axial rotation differs from orbital revolution.

Why, my dear reader, the only reason why the moon is a satellite is because she has lost her power to rotate on her own axis.

If she could be rejuvenated by an atmosphere, she would be startled into motion by solar heat; its pressure and motion would create axial rotation; axial rotation would beget orbital revolution around the sun, as of yore.

But if axial rotation originated orbital revolution, how does the moon maintain orbital motion without axial rotation?

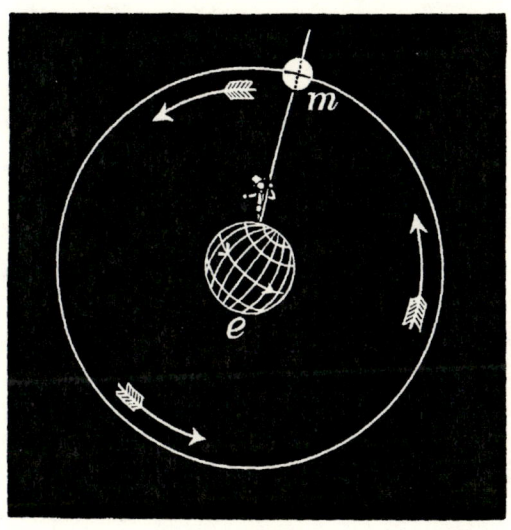

FIG. 14.

Furthermore, why is her orbit around the earth instead of around the sun?

When the moon had an atmosphere, her orbit was around the sun. When she lost her atmosphere, she lost her orbital motor: but, notwithstanding, she continued her orbital motion, consequent upon the prior *impulse* she had already received from her atmospheric pressure and motion during its existence. Having lost her rotatory motor, and with it her orbital motor, she now moves in her orbit in obedience to forces explained by Sir Isaac Newton, as the result of a *primitive impulse*. We have previously shown where and how this impulse was obtained.

184   PHILOSOPHY OF PHENOMENA.

When the moon lost her orbital motor and depended wholly upon the momentum derived from the former impulse, she lazily continued motion in her old orbit until she came in conjunction with a sister planet whose attraction was exerted upon

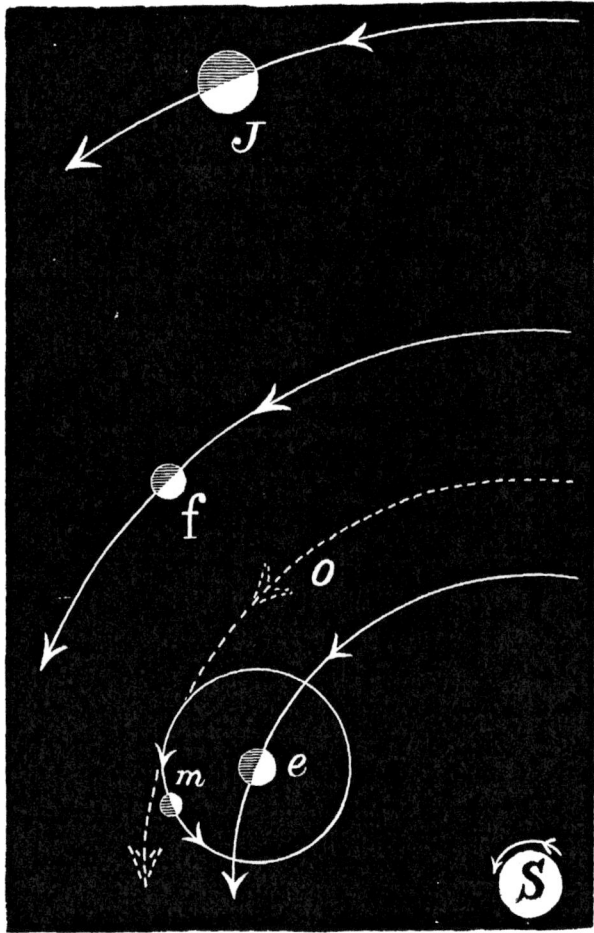

FIG. 15.

her with more potency than the sun's; whereupon, she was constrained to retire from attendance upon her old monarch and do homage to the earth.

Some writers on astronomy tell us that the sun attracts the moon with two and one-half times greater power than the earth does; and yet, in the face of this reckless assertion, the earth annually drags the moon around an orbit of 600,000,000 miles; while the moon travels 17,280,000 miles on her own resources, and passes between the sun and earth twelve times annually, never showing any disposition to skip toward the sun.

In Fig. 15, we have attempted to show how the earth became master of the moon; wherein S represents the sun, e the earth, f Mars, J Jupiter, m the moon, and o the moon's old orbit around the sun. The moon having lost her orbital motor, was consequently moving wholly by the momentum impulse originally obtained from her lost motor.

The resistant medium in which she moved was too minute to arrest her motion, and the sun's attraction was too minute to overcome her orbital centrifugal force; consequently, when she came in conjunction with the earth, other planets being favorably situated to check her orbital motion, the earth was able to gain entire control, whereupon the moon became servant to a sister planet.

The moon's original orbit around the sun was evidently exterior to the earth's orbit; otherwise her orbital motion would have been the reverse of what it is.

The earth, doubtless, had a conflict with Mars and the mighty Jupiter ere she won the prize.

It is difficult to describe, and impossible to show by drawings, the moon's true path around the earth, owing to the different orbital velocities of earth and moon. However, it is known that, owing to the earth's great orbital velocity and large orbit, as compared with the moon's orbital velocity and orbit, that the moon's path is always concave toward the sun, notwithstanding she passes between the earth and sun during each lunation; and although she makes a complete revolution around the earth, her path, as delineated on the ecliptic, describes less than one-eighth of a circle. Furthermore, the moon's path is uniform in its curve; never retrogrades; shows no sharp turns, as represented in many text-books.

CHAPTER XXXVI.

ETHNOLOGICAL PHENOMENA

ETHNOLOGY is a term used to designate a science that makes the study of man a specialty.

The climax of all man's thoughts and aspirations culminates in a desire to obtain a knowledge of his own origin and destiny.

To learn whence he came and whither he goeth is his constant yearning.

All of literature, all of art, all of science, all of life, concentres in the one intense inquiry of man's origin, brotherhood and destiny.

The origin of man is strangely more obscure than his destiny. His obscurity of origin arises from his dense ignorance at the time of his advent; while a better knowledge of his destiny arises from his acquisition of knowledge since his advent, and because man can reason more correctly prospectively than he can retrospectively.

It is the general drift of scientific thought at present, that man is the result of evolution from the crudest form of animate being.

Some of our most eminent scientists have come to the conclusion that the origin of man and of worlds is the same; that both originated from nebulous matter. Thence they argue that the mineral, the vegetable and the animal kingdoms differ only in evolutionary degrees; that the nebula itself had a primordial existence in an invisible gaseous form; that the primary change was from the invisible gaseous state to the visible nebulous state; that all we now behold in the heavens above and on and in the earth beneath, including the waters thereof, results from a succession of changes of the gaseous matter that once pervaded all space.

Some scientists go so far as to ascribe even thought *per se* to the result of highly organized matter, culminating in man.

The advocates of such belief are known as materialists, in contra-distinction from an opposite class known as spiritualists. Then again, there is an intermediate class known as theists, who inadvertently preach and practise both — who, however strange it may seem, are more zealous in cursing spiritualism than materialism; who are too stupid to perceive that Theos is spirit, that spirit is life, that thought can only proceed from life, that life, spirit and Theos are one and the same, while matter and materialism are wholly different.

Those materialistic scientists who believe that life and thought are the result of highly organic forms of matter also believe that when the organic body perishes, life and thought perish with the body.

The fallacy of this conclusion has been fully shown elsewhere; suffice it to remark here, that inasmuch as matter is indestructible, it follows that all its properties are also indestructible; and as mind is cumulative, it is more potent to maintain existence and to effect a subsequent re-organization with matter than in the original.

Man is emphatically a spirit.

This body which you see — so many feet high and so many pounds weight — is not I.

The most profound thinker ever born on this continent (Dr. Franklin) held "that man is not a body animated, but rather an animate spirit clothed with a body."

This material body which you see is but the place wherein I dwell and through which I manifest. When my coat becomes worn and no longer fitted for use, I lay it off and don another. So, too, with my body: when it becomes unfitted for my habitation, I creep out and build me another that is habitable. I ever remaining invisible, my new body also becomes invisible to normal vision.

However, it is not my purpose to dwell at length upon man as a spirit; but we deemed this much necessary in order that, during this discussion of the subject, the house might not be mistaken for the proprietor. Hereafter we may in some instances speak of man corporeal, in the language of common parlance; we must not, however, treat man, either in his corporeal or spiritual character, as different from other animals, except only in respect of his higher degree of excellence in knowledge.

Science has traced matter in regular gradations from the nebulous condition up to its incorporation with man.

Matter has been traced from the nebulæ to the meteor, from the meteor to the comet; from the comet to the planet, with its rocks and minerals and oceans. Science finds substance that is part mineral, part vegetable; again, we find substance that is a combination of vegetable and animal, that puzzles naturalists to tell whether the substance is animal or vegetable. Thence science has traced animate life through thousands of shades and degrees of evolution — from the amœba to the radiates, to the mollusks, to the articulates, and finally to the vertebrates, in which the fish represents the lowest and man the highest; and in which are included many intermediate classes of the monkey family, making a chain with but few links yet to be placed.

This progressive development theory is generally known as the Darwinian theory. The theory is not wholly original with him. Much of the fundamental basis he found prepared by others. Nevertheless, he made the theory of evolution a specialty, and cleared away more rubbish by which it was environed than all others; and it may justly bear his name.

In confirmation of this theory, Professor Huxley claims to have demonstrated that the origin of life manifestations is the very same in the vegetable and animal.

Now, if man in his corporeal capacity is but matter vitalized by life, it becomes an exceeding interesting inquiry to ascertain his antiquity, to learn in what geological period man, as such, made his *début* on the surface of *terra firma*.

It is also interesting to learn what manner of man he came forth. Was he white, red, yellow or black? Which of the four general divisions was the original? And which are the varieties?

In order to arrive at a logical conclusion in regard to these inquiries, it is necessary to inquire first, what was the earliest geological period in which the earth could sustain man in his organic form.

The science of paleontology teaches that in the carboniferous period air-breathing animals existed in great abundance; that both carnivorous and herbivorous lived during that period. Man being omnivorous, no doubt he, too, lived at that early period. Who can tell how many thousands of years since?

Agassiz called the carboniferous period the summer period; consequent upon the great abundance of vegetable and animal products that existed during that period. The immense vegetable and animal production of the carboniferous period is evidence of a warm period. A warm period results from a small orbit. The laws that govern the construction of orbits, together with the motions of planets, show that the earth at some indefinite period of time suddenly changed the geographical positions of her polar centre to the extent of twenty or more degrees; whereby a new orbit in shape and area was created.

If this displacement of polar centre occurs when the earth is at her aphelion, her orbit is greatly enlarged; if the change occurs when the earth is at her perihelion, her orbit is greatly reduced in area. And thus it "came to pass" that the carboniferous period was smaller, consequently warmer, than either the preceding or succeeding periods.

We are now prepared to ask whether the white, red or black man is most in harmony with this excessively hot period?

We might further ask, Which is the superior people? and further remind you, that the order of development, away back and down to the silurian period, as shown by fossillized animals, has always been from the lower to the higher (Hackel).

Now, you already anticipate the original.

All know that the negro is emphatically a creature best adapted to a warm climate.

Indeed, we can prove from a scientific basis, that the dark skin of the negro is a direct result of a warm climate such as existed during the carboniferous period.

By chemical analysis it is found that the black matter (*pigmentum nigrum*) situated in the integument of the negro is almost pure carbon.

Carbon is a poor conductor of heat; hence its use as a protector from undue heat consequent upon a small orbit. However, carbon was not a material selected from nature's store by any intellectual effort; the carbon protector was wholly a result of physical operations. While life urged by sensation struggled to maintain its organic habitation in flesh, the sun burned and baked the carbon crust upon the surface, whereby the organism was better adapted to the environment, and the struggle rendered less urgent.

Again, the peculiar curly kinky hair of the negro is a result of the same cause that originally produced the carbon crust upon his surface.

The color of the hair of all varieties of the race is dependent upon the same kind of pigment. The only difference is in quality and quantity.

The epidermis (top skin) of all people is composed of epidermic cells, which become flattened and dried and hardened by exposure. And mixed up with these dermic cells are the pigment cells, or granules. The hair is but a modification — a prolongation — of these dermic and pigment cells.

The black matter is developed within the follicle, whence the hair is projected, and it is absorbed by the little dermic cells of which the hair is formed.

Now, if the white-skinned variety of the race is susceptible to the development of this pigment as coloring for the hair, it is easily seen that the black-skinned variety would be more susceptible and would develop a greater abundance. An increase of pigment is an increase of carbon; the more carbon, the darker the hair; the more abundant the pigment cells, the more compact; and the more compact, the more flattened they become upon being wedged up against each other and between the dermic cells of which the hair proper is constituted; the flatter the cells, the flatter the hair and the more kinky.

Round hair is always straight, and flat hair is always curly or kinky. It is true that we sometimes find hair curly, but never kinky, except on the head of an aged negro.

Some take much satisfaction in calling the negroes' hair "wool." The division line where hair ceases and wool begins, we leave to hair-splitting philosophers.

We next invite attention to an explanation of the origin of varieties of race.

We have seen that the negro is truly a carbon man, resulting from environment, consequent upon intense heat, which always implies light; that this intense heat and light were the results of a small orbit; and that, as a sequence, the whole race at that time were negroes.

Now, in order to produce a variety of the race, it was necessary to change the entire conditions of environment relative to both heat and light.

This requisite change occurred when the earth changed the location of her polar centres, as elsewhere explained; whereby the orbit became enlarged and the old tropics became suddenly situated in the arctic regions. This sudden change from a torrid to a frigid climate caused the necessity of clothing, to cover the carbonized skin — now a detriment. The covering prevented the radiation of heat, now so essential, and also shut out the light (although it was not so intense or constant as formerly); consequently the carbon was slowly and gradually eliminated, the original cause of its production and necessity being abrogated in degree.

The ancient cave-dwellers, found in this country and Europe, were people who were forced to seek caves for shelter and protection from the intense cold to which they were suddenly and unexpectedly exposed. And as ages rolled away, the *pigmentum nigrum* became eliminated, the inhabitants of cold regions bleached to many shades and degrees of color; and, lo, the red and yellow man walks the earth!

The antiquity of man is no doubt very great; he doubtless was a cotemporary of the mastodon and three-toed horse.

In California, near Cherokee Village, there are ancient ruins, supposed to be 180,000 years old.

A few years since there was a human skull found in volcanic rock, under Table Mountain (California), supposed to have been deposited during the miocene or eocene ages (Lesquereux).

At the close of the carboniferous period, the so-called tertiary period was ushered in, whereby the earth's orbit was further enlarged, and thus made more favorable for the further elimination of carbon from the integument of man.

It is impossible for any one to assign even a proximate number of years designating the length of any geological period; however, many phenomena are found which go to show that the tertiary period was one of long duration.

As already shown, a reconstruction of axis becomes a necessity consequent upon its extreme inclination. The axes of all the planets are constantly changing their degrees of inclination, from the same cause affecting the earth.

The earth's rate of axial decrease is about one-half a second annually.

Laplace has shown that this decrease must continue — provided all external influences remain as at present — until the axis becomes perpendicular, when it will again resume its inclination, the limit of which he has not stated.

The earth's present degree of axial inclination is given at 23° 27′ 8″. With its present rate of decrease, it will require about 16,900 years to bring the axis to a perpendicular. Then, with the same rate of increase, it will require about

324,000 years to bring the axis down to an inclination of 45°, its extreme limit. Thence we may reasonably infer that the tertiary period continued more than 300,000 years: if a man was incorporated with matter during the entire period, what may have been the number of the race when the present period was ushered in?

If 400 years gives a white population of 65,000,000 to America, 300,000 years would give a population of 48,750,000,000, without considering the per cent. rate of increase.

Under such environments, unless in the mean time immense changes have occurred from the present environment, a reconstruction of axis would be supremely desirable.

The comparatively few human inhabitants found in America, when first discovered by Columbus, is *prima facie* evidence that the larger part of this continent was submerged during the last great deluge; also that the deluge must have occurred only a few thousand years since.

Having wandered from anthropoidal subject proper, we now return to make a finish, with but few further considerations, and remark, first, that a continuation of the cause that produced the red variety of race, together with an increased degree of potency, would and did produce the white variety.

It is found by chemical analysis that the freckle of the white man is the very same as the *pigmentum nigrum* of the negro. Both are almost pure carbon.

All are conversant with the fact, that during winter, when the sun's rays are less effective, when we are well clothed and well housed, the freckles disappear, consequent upon the diminished light and heat of the sun. But when the bright warm April sun shines, the freckles again appear; thus evidencing the blood from whence we were bred; also our true lineage; and I hope we are worthy descendants of our grand old ancestors of the carboniferous period and carbon hue.

Darwin avers that all fauna and flora have an inherent tendency, when the least encouraged by environment, to revert to the original type. Thence the facility with which the white man elaborates the freckles is incontrovertible evidence that the colored man was his original.

This facility to freckle and tan, together with the extensive torrid zone of the present period, show that present conditions are amply sufficient to perpetuate the production of black men without the aid of the carboniferous period.

Thus we find that the negro is father to the red and yellow varieties and grandfather to the white variety.

But we are told that the negro has enjoyed the benefit of the white man's climate in America for nearly four hundred years, and yet shows no signs of decarbonizing.

Four hundred years is very short when compared with one axial period; and yet, even in this short period, we are not without evidence that the negro is amenable to the decarbonizing influence by which he is at present environed.

In Harrisburg, Pa., there lives an old negress verging unto one hundred, whose skin is a light creamy mulatto, with long straight hair; whereas, when a young girl, she was jet black, with black, kinky hair. Quite recently a case is reported in Florida, of a colored man who became white in one spot, which enlarged until his whole body is now much too light for a mulatto. Why, there is no law so irrevocable as the law that like causes produce like results.

When we contemplate the antiquity of the negro, the perils by which he has been surrounded and through which he has survived, he becomes truly venerable in the estimation of historians and all who revere age and heroism. Again, when we fully realize his innocence as author of his own color, and the millions of kicks and curses received and borne from his own more fortunate offspring, we feel that every Biblical nation, and every individual by whom he has thus been punished without cause should hang their heads in very shame when in the presence of their grand old ancestors.

CHAPTER XXXVII.

THE COLORED MAN.

No phenomenon of nature has given rise to more balderdash or gross manifestations of ignorance than the colored variety of men.

Orthodoxy, the synonym of bigotry and ignorance, holds that the negro is the result of an old drunk who cursed his grandchildren before they were born. Could anything be more silly?

Heretofore we have shown that every phenomenon, including every variety and degree, results primarily from physical operations, modified by the interposition of life.

Were it not for physical operations, life phenomena could never have existed.

Thus we learn that physical phenomena constitute the very bed rock on which and from which all metaphysical phenomena evolve to recognition.

The negro *per se* is wholly the result of climatic influence. So, too, is the white man.

As time rolls on, the inherent forces of matter, ever operative, will again and again diversify climate over the whole earth. In time the black man of the Congo will become environed by the same conditions as the white man of America; in short, their present conditions will be reversed.

As like causes always produce like results, it follows that the black and white man will exchange wool for hair and hair for wool; the black man will fade to white, and the white man will ebonize; and there will be no help for it until another climatic change reverses their conditions.

But we are told by superficial thinkers that the negro has had the benefit of a white man's climate in America for four hundred years, and yet remains black. Oh, how insignificant are four hundred years, when compared with a polar period of one hundred to three hundred thousand years' duration!

And yet we are not without evidence of the bleaching influence of four hundred years, elsewhere shown.

In view of the inevitable operations of matter resulting from irrevocable forces resident therein, how childish it is for white men to boast of a superiority originating wholly from fortuitous environment, over which man has had not the least control.

In America, while this slow but sure evolution of the black man to the white variety is in progress, under the law of environment, there are other agents at work, equally potent and vastly more speedy in their bleaching results.

The trend of events is toward equalization of all classes.

The flood tide of tyranny, of usurpation, of caste, has reached its limit. Education is the great emancipator of all.

The colored people of the United States maintain seven colleges, seventeen academies and fifty high schools.

Education levels both up and down.

One day it elevates and enthrones the flat-boatmen of the Sangamon to be the ruler of the greatest people on earth; on another day it dethrones the Emperor Dom Pedro to the level of the people.

Education is slowly but surely dethroning all monarchical governments, and dissolving all hierarchical bodies.

Thomas Jefferson's sublime declaration, that "all men have equal rights to life, liberty and the pursuit of happiness," has become the beacon of the world.

Intelligence, morals and possessions determine the status of all. Each and all result from special environment. Under the potency of education and wealth, miscenegation is evolved with the same assurance that summer sunshine and showers evolve fruits and flowers.

Already on this continent there are several colored millionnaires who are waited upon by white men and maidens.[1]

Despite of present malace, miscenegation will solve the race problem on this continent within the next century.

Let us cease to fight against the inevitable — against irrevocable environments that evolve morals in harmony therewith.

"Let us have peace," now, upon the broad basis of equal rights under the very same laws. Let this be our standard. Let each individual find his own level without hindrance. Let all recognize and respect the status thus gained. The one great question with the American people is, Shall the sublime declaration of equal rights stand or fall? That is the culmination of all good men's aspirations.

Who art thou, O fortuitous arrogant, who sayeth nay to the necessitous ones who are tyrannized by love of life in the flesh, and who yearn for food, raiment and shelter?

Rejoice, O brethren, that race antagonism is dying; it is dying hard, but its death is certain.

Already many whites and blacks and *creamies* have intermarried. The affinity of the two, as evidenced by procreation, proves the oneness, the unity of the race. Within the present century, a white woman in South Carolina gave birth to twins — one white and one black. "Homogeneity" was herein demonstrated beyond controversy.

Already there are in America one hundred thousand people in whom an Agassiz could not tell whether the white or black blood predominated.

---

[1] THE SOUTH'S THRIFTY NEGROES. — "Recent reports in regard to the acquisition of property by negroes are surprising to many who have not carefully watched the march of events," says the Jacksonville (Fla.) *Citizen*. On Emancipation Day the statement was made in a public address at Memphis, Tenn., that the negroes in the thirteen Southern States, including Missouri, and leaving out Maryland and Delaware, pay taxes on $136,300,000 worth of property, the largest amount being owned in Louisiana, to the value of $18,000,000, and the smallest in Virginia, to the amount of $4,900,000. Texas shows $18,000,-000, Mississippi $13,400,000, South Carolina $12,500,000, North Carolina $11,-000,000, Georgia and Tennessee each $10,400,000, Alabama $9,200,000, Arkansas $8,000,000, Florida $7,900,000, Missouri $6,600,000, Kentucky $5,900,000.

And yet we have blatant statesmen, very reverend bishops, and arrogant scientists, who insist that there is an impassable gulf between the white and the colored man, ordained by God.

The affiliation of the two varieties is so strong, so natural, that the ethics of society, statute law, the shotgun and religious fervor are all powerless to prevent miscenegation.

O arrogant man, creature of cosmic force and chance environment, cease to fight against the inevitable!

Indulgent reader — and others — here we rest, and await the verdict of ages.

APPENDIX.

The following problems were respectfully submitted for solution to those pre-eminent scientists whose courteous answers are herewith appended, to all of whom we extend unbounded thanks.

All of their solutions are unqualified confirmations of the theory expounded in this volume, namely, that the motion of the Earth's aerial envelope originated and perpetuates the earth's diurnal rotation.

PROBLEMS.

Given a globe one foot in diameter, inclosed in an envelope that exerts one pound of pressure upon every square inch of globe surface, if the envelope is made to revolve in any direction, will the globe revolve in the same direction? If not, why not?

Again, given a globe 90,000 miles in diameter, inclosed in an envelope that exerts thirty pounds of pressure upon every square inch of globe surface, the question is, If the envelope is made to revolve in any direction, will the globe revolve in the same direction? If not, why not?

SMITHSONIAN INSTITUTION,
WASHINGTON, D. C., January 11, 1896.

DEAR SIR:— In reply to your letter of January 6th, containing the statement of a problem in mechanics, I beg leave to say that, if I understand your problem aright, the tendency of a rotating envelope upon a spherical globe, not subject to the disturbance of other forces, would be to communicate its motion of revolution to the globe itself, whether the globe be one foot in diameter, as in your first question, or ninety thousand miles in diameter, in the second. The motion of the globe tends to the same direction as the motion of its envelope.

Very respectfully yours,   S. P. LANGLEY, *Secretary*.

COLUMBIA COLLEGE, NEW YORK, January 23, 1896.

DEAR SIR:—President Low having handed over to me your letter of January 21st, I would state, that if an envelope surrounding a globe of any dimensions and exerting on it any pressure whatsoever, be set and kept in rotation, it will sooner or later cause the globe itself to rotate in the same direction and with the same velocity.

Very truly yours,   OGDEN N. ROOD,
Professor of Physics in Columbia College.

OBERLIN, O., January 30, 1896.

GEORGE M. RAMSEY, M.D. *Dear Sir:*—Your favor of the 20th inst. is received. In reply to your questions, I would say that I see no reason why the globes which you describe should not both revolve in the direction in which the envelopes do. If the fact is otherwise, I should be glad to know it.   Very truly yours,

G. F. WRIGHT.

BROWN UNIVERSITY, PROVIDENCE,
February 28, 1896.

MR. G. M. RAMSEY. *Dear Sir:*—Dr. Andrews has handed me yours of the 19th inst., and requested me to answer you.

Your two questions are identical, and the same answer applies to both.

If the surface of the globe is perfectly smooth, so that there is no friction between it and the medium, it will remain at rest, however the envelope be moved, since there is no force tending to turn it. On the other hand, if its surface be perfectly rough, so that there can be no slipping between envelope and globe, the globe will turn with the envelope When the surface is imperfectly rough, that is, when the coefficient of friction between globe and envelope is not infinite, the globe will begin to move slowly at the same time the envelope starts, and will gradually attain the same velocity as the envelope, the time occupied depending on the mass of the globe and the normal pressure of the envelope, increasing with the former and decreasing with the latter.

Yours truly,   A. DeF. PALMER, Jr., Ph.D.

APPENDIX. 201

Mr. G. M. Ramsey. *Dear Sir:* — President Eliot has referred your letter to me for an answer. If the "envelope" is any ordinary solid, liquid, or gas, both of your questions must be answered, Yes. There may be such a thing as a frictionless substance, but we cannot be said to be sure upon that point now.

Very truly yours, Edwin H. Hall,
Professor of Physics, Harvard College.

Johns Hopkins University, Baltimore, March 6, 1896.

Dear Sir: — President Gilman asks me to say that your note of February 25th has been referred to one of the mathematical gentlemen here, who makes the following statement:

"The answers depend entirely upon whether there is friction between the envelope and the globe, or not. If there is any friction, no matter how small, the motion of the envelope will in each case produce motion of the globe. If there is no friction, this is not true."

Yours truly, T. R. Ball, *Registrar.*

New Haven, March 9, 1896.

Mr. Geo. M Ramsey. *Dear Sir:* — In reply to your recent letter to Pres. Dwight, which has been handed to me to answer, I would say that it depends on the manner in which we may suppose the pressure to be exerted. If, as a matter of theoretical abstraction, we imagine the pressure to be "*frictionless,*" such a pressure would not make the sphere revolve, but in a practical case, if the envelope was a solid pressing on the sphere, or a fluid pressing on the sphere, the friction or viscosity (even a gas would have a certain amount of viscosity) would exert a force to make the sphere revolve. The size of the sphere might retard the motion, but could not prevent it.

Very respectfully yours, J. W. Gibbs.

Clokey, Pa., March 2, 1896.

James B. Ansell, LL.D. *Dear Sir:* — Kindly oblige me by expressing an opinion upon the following problems in which I am deeply interested.

Given a globe one foot in diameter inclosed in an envelope that exerts one pound of pressure upon every square inch of globe surface. Question: If the envelope is made to revolve in any direction, will the globe revolve in the same direction? If not, why not?

[It would revolve in the same direction unless the globe is perfectly smooth.]

Again, given a globe 80,000 miles in diameter, inclosed in an envelope that exerts thirty pounds of pressure upon every square inch of globe surface, the question again is, If the envelope is made to revolve in any direction, will the globe revolve in the same direction? If not, why not?

[Same as above.]

Awaiting your pleasure, I have the honor to remain,

    Truly yours,   GEO. M. RAMSEY.

The above letter was forwarded by President Ansell to Mr. Hall of the Observatory at Ann Arbor, Mich., whose replies were noted on the letter itself, as shown by the clauses enclosed in brackets.

    STANFORD UNIVERSITY, CAL., March 12, 1896.

DEAR SIR:— Your letter of the 2d March, containing two questions regarding the action of spheres surrounded by envelopes in rotation, has been referred to me.

I have no hesitation in answering both of your questions in the affirmative, provided there be friction between the sphere and its envelope. Yours truly, R. E. ALLARDELL.

    UNITED STATES DEPARTMENT OF AGRICULTURE,
    OFFICE OF CHIEF OF WEATHER BUREAU,
    WASHINGTON, D. C., April 10, 1896.

MR. GEO. M. RAMSEY, Clokey, Pa.

DEAR SIR:— In reply to your letter of the 2d instant, addressed to the Honorable J. Sterling Morton, Secretary of Agriculture, I have the pleasure to inform you that cyclones usually move eastward in the temperate zones, but westward in the tropics, as for example, the West Indian hurricanes before they recurve near the Gulf States. The easterly moving storms must necessarily have a greater angular velocity about the earth's axis of rotation, since they move faster than the surface of the earth immediately beneath them.

    Very respectfully, WILLIS L. MOORE,
              Chief of Bureau.

            April 28, 1896.

PROF. WILLIS L. MOORE, *Chief of Weather Bureau, Washington, D. C.*

DEAR SIR:— I again thank you for favor of 2d inst., also for permission to print.

I further wish to express my delight in learning that the weather bureaus of the world have agreed to spend one year in surveying clouds. Clouds, and clouds only, tell exactly which way and how fast the wind goes. Doubtless, many meteorological heresies will be dispelled thereby; meanwhile, I am exceedingly anxious that the Washington Bureau shall excel all others, and venture to predict the following discoveries:

(1) That an east wind never existed.

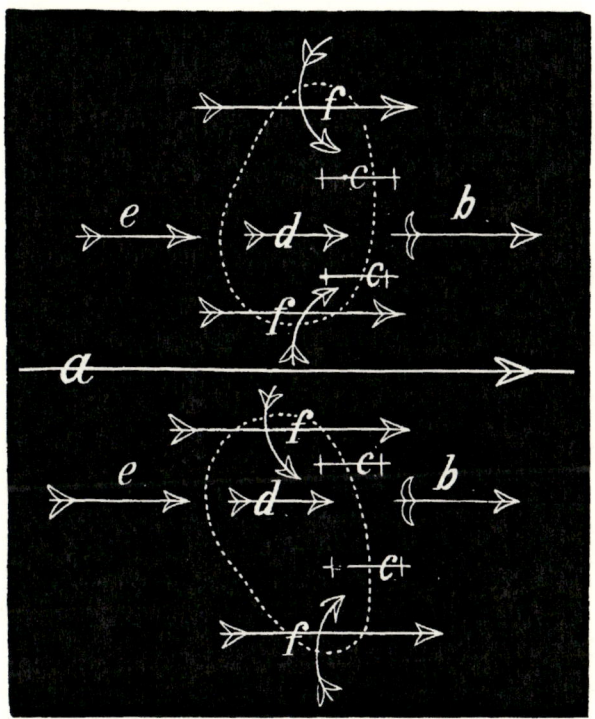

(2) That air currents circulating from the equator toward the poles have no existence.

(3) That the normal circulation of the air is toward the east (the sun), and always crosses the line of illumination at right angles.

(4) Although air motion is always eastward, it may and does ofttimes diverge northward and southward, notwithstanding its eastward velocity continues much the greater.

(5) That the angular eastward velocity of the great aerial ocean is always greater than the earth's velocity of rotation; that trade-winds (so-called), tropical cyclones and all others, move eastward.

(6) Apart from electrical disturbances, storms always result from

204   APPENDIX.

air having a much greater or much less velocity of motion in the same or divergent direction of the earth's rotation; consequently, a calm results from the air and the earth having the same velocity of motion in the same direction.

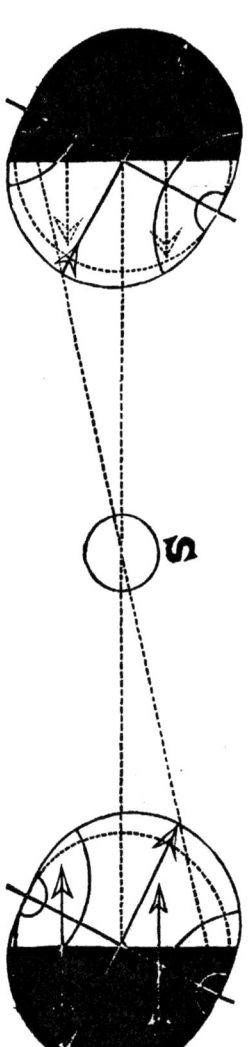

(7) That low areas always move eastward; always retard air motion eastward of the low, and accelerate air motion westward of the low; while immediately north and south of the low, the air is made to diverge toward the low, consequently partakes of a compound motion.

The writer cannot refrain from venturing the statement, that a majority of meteorologists fail to comprehend the legitimate motions of misnamed cyclones, inasmuch as they never complete a cycle (circle).

Cyclonic motions result from large areas of low pressure, ofttimes a thousand miles or more in diameter, and usually much larger in the north and south dimensions than in the east and west; while the boundaries nearest the temperate zones are usually in advance, owing to the influence of the calm belt at or near the equator.

The diagram on page 203 shows the true cyclonic motions; *a* represents the equator. The spaces within the dotted lines represent low areas. The arrows indicate the direction of the wind; they also indicate different velocities.

That diagram also shows why the wind in the northern hemisphere appears to move like the hands on a clock (when facing north), and the reverse in the southern hemisphere.

Arrows *b* indicate less air motion than the earth's velocity of rotation; arrows *c* indicate a region wherein air and earth have the same velocity, consequently a calm; arrows *d* indicate air motion a little faster than the earth; arrows *e* indicate air motion faster than arrows *d*; arrows *f* indicate the cyclonic compound motion of the air.

Although somewhat irrelevant to the subject under consideration, I wish to add, that every motion of the earth results from solar heat and solar attraction. Solar heat is the sole factor of air motion, resulting in diurnal and orbital motions.

The wabble of the earth's poles results from the unequal pull of the atmosphere and the sun, alternately upon the poles and equator, when the earth is at opposite solstices; whereas the pull is equal only when the earth is at equinoxes. Consequently when the axis become perpendicular to the plane of her orbit, the wabble will be imperceptible. See diagram on page 204, representing the earth at both solstices; arrows showing the direction of the earth's rotation and the normal direction of air motion. Yours respectfully,
GEO. M. RAMSEY.

PHYSICAL AND METAPHYSICAL PHENOMENA, *AD INFINITUM.*

> " Our good friend Huxley can't tell why ducks lay eggs;
> Nor how stumbled into them, wings and legs." —LONGFELLOW.

YES, by the logic of evolution, Huxley can tell why ducks lay eggs, and how stumbled into them, wings and legs; but the answer does not come by one leap, like jumping a ditch.

We must first recognize the stern fact, that all phenomena are exactly what environment has made them: that environment is infinite in variety and degree. Hence, to give an intelligent answer, we must go back, and start with the first faint glimmer of life, as perceived in the germ-plasm, in the unicell, and trace its slow and almost imperceptible evolution, by multiplication of cells into complex organisms; whence we eventually arrive at ducks and eggs, with wings and legs.

Our first premise toward a solution of this most interesting problem is, that matter and life are self-existent: are co-existent throughout eternity, including the past and future.

Matter and life being indestructible, these premises are logically evident; indeed, are self-evident. Hence, it is logical to further assume that matter and life are distinct factors, are the sole factors of all phenomena; that all phenomena result from differentiated unions of these two; that, inasmuch as matter is constantly changing its molecular relations within itself, and as every change necessitates a differentiated union, therefore, differentiated manifestations of life must ensue.

Hence, again, if we further consider the infinite duration of matter and life, together with their inevitable differentiated re-unions in kind and degree, *ad infinitum*, it is seen that ducks and eggs, with wings and legs, are inevitable.

Matter and life being distinctive factors, each possesses distinctive attributes and properties not possessed by the other. Two inherent and dominant forces found in matter are attraction and repulsion, in constant warfare; whereby molecular polarity momentarily changes their relations, giving rise to physical phenomena — scismic and meteorologic — wherein life has no part or prophecy whatsoever. But life is wholly unable to manifest in any form without the aid of matter. Thus it would seem that matter is paramount. But when we consider the transcendent characteristics of phenomena wherein life is the conspicuous factor, we are forced to concede that life is supreme.

Every manifestation of life is through matter, and imparts to each atom through which it manifests, an impress that is perpetual, which renders each atom more susceptible to a subsequent impress; and thus life ever urges progressive evolution from the amœba to man.

Although matter is easily resolved from the solid to the liquid and gaseous conditions, and the reverse, yet it never again returns to exact previous conditions; hence continuous evolution results in differentiated phenomena.

The term Nature, in its broad and truly legitimate sense, includes all that is: includes matter and life in all their varied attributes and manifestations. But, notwithstanding, she is limited in her operations by conditions that are constantly changing; consequently she can have no forecast and works towards no ideal. She never designed an octopus, a toad, a tumble-bug; never designed a humming-bird, a peacock, or transcendent woman — pearl of the universe. Nor may these be considered accidental phenomena *per se*. All, however, are legitimate results of an accidental environment that is constantly changing, and is thus thwarting results that otherwise would have occurred. Thus we find that all her evolutions of higher phenomena result from incessant warfare of inherent, insensate forces of matter, in the form of attraction and repulsion of molecules wholly void of volition — modified, however, in some cases by life's previous impress on matter, as varied conditions have permitted.

Possibly every atom of earth has received life's impress; therefore, every subsequent impress only modifies previous impresses; and hence, in this age, we perceive evolution on old lines.

Huxley has shown, that so far as chemical or microscopical tests can determine, the incipient formation of the protoplastic cellule is the very same in the vegetate and animate; but as one develops the vegetate and the other the animate, it follows that one had received the invisible vegetate impress, and the other the animate impress. Life being invisible, it may not seem strange that life's initial impress may also be invisible.

Bear in mind, that different impressions result wholly from the different conditions in which matter existed when the impress was given.

Time infinite implies conditions infinite. Infinite conditions imply infinite kinds and degrees of impression, and consequently infinite differentiated phenomena.

Botanists recognize more than three hundred thousand species of plants. Zoölogists recognize more than two million differentiated animate forms; doubtless, there are other trillions yet unknown.

Now, inasmuch as evolution has superseded the special creation delusion, it follows that classification of flora and fauna into species and genera is wholly inadmissible. The logic of evolution teaches that all are included under the term *varieties;* that, from the unicell to complex man, all life manifestations are but modifications of the primal protoplasm. Consequently, one type includes all.

Matter and life being the only known agents of phenomena, it follows without the saying, that all life manifestations are but evolutions of the primal unicell.

Life ever and continuously strives to express itself, whether conditions are favorable or not.

When conditions are favorable, expressions are lovely, are good; when unfavorable, expressions are bad, are hideous, ofttimes pernicious.

Why this constant struggle of life, under all conditions, to express its ubiquity, we know not. No more do we know why either life or matter exists. These are terminal chasms none may cross; these are terminal stations where all stop off. There is nothing beyond.

Printed in the United States
23057LVS00004B/305